# WALKS INTO

# DORSET

## John Wilks

COUNTRYSIDE BOOKS

NEWBURY BERKSHIRE

COUNTRYSIDE BOOKS
3 Catherine Road
Newbury, Berkshire

To view our complete range of books,
please visit us at
www.countrysidebooks.co.uk

ISBN 978 1 84674 033 6

Photographs by the author

Designed by Peter Davies, Nautilus Design

Produced through MRM Associates Ltd., Reading
Typeset by Jean Cussons Typesetting, Diss, Norfolk
Printed by Cambridge University Press

# Contents

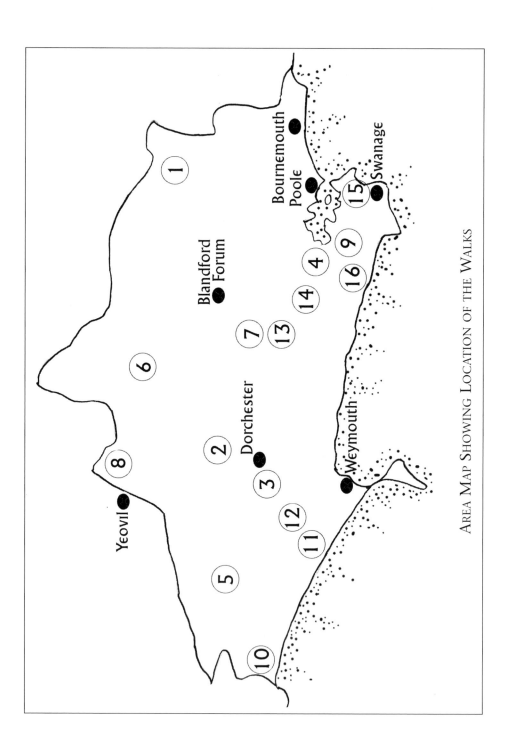

AREA MAP SHOWING LOCATION OF THE WALKS

WALK

PUBLISHER'S NOTE

We hope that you obtain considerable enjoyment from this book; great care has been taken in its preparation. Although at the time of publication all routes followed public rights of way or permitted paths, diversion orders can be made and permissions withdrawn.

We cannot, of course, be held responsible for such diversion orders and any inaccuracies in the text which result from these or any other changes to the routes nor any damage which might result from walkers trespassing on private property. We are anxious though that all details covering the walks are kept up to date and would therefore welcome information from readers which would be relevant to future editions.

The simple sketch maps that accompany the walks in this book are based on notes made by the author whilst checking out the routes on the ground. However, for the benefit of a proper map, we do recommend that you purchase the relevant Ordnance Survey sheet covering your walk. The Ordnance Survey maps are widely available, especially through booksellers and local newsagents.

# INTRODUCTION

Wherever you walk in Dorset there are fascinating reminders of past lives and events. Add this to the beauty and peace of the countryside and you have a recipe for some great days out in this wonderful county of sweeping downland, rich pastures, shady woods and spectacular cliffs and beaches.

Each walk in this book is accompanied by a commentary on what is unfolding around you, which adds so much to the experience. A walk on the ramparts of majestic Maiden Castle is enhanced by discovering how and where the Roman legions defeated the local inhabitants in bloody battle nearly 2,000 years ago. Or a pleasant stroll along the coast can uncover the activities of the Moonfleet smugglers in the shelter of Chesil Beach in the 18th century. Set out in chronological order, the walks can take you from the Stone Age Knowlton Rings, to the preparations for D-Day in 1944 played out on the lovely beaches of Studland Bay, each route highlighting a particular moment in our history.

Many of the walks are on fairly flat terrain but there are a few with a climb or two – no problem when, for instance, the result is to enjoy magnificent views from Swyre Head over Kimmeridge Bay. All are circular and grid references are given for the starting point. Sketch maps are included for your guidance but, for more detail, it is strongly recommended that you carry the appropriate Ordnance Survey map. Convenient parking places have been noted for each walk, most of them free of charge, but please park at all times with consideration for other road users and take care not to block any exits or entrances.

There is a note in each chapter indicating where refreshments can be obtained, but it is always advisable to carry a drink and snack with you, particularly on the longer walks. Remember also, that at certain times of the year, paths can be muddy or brambles and nettles may have grown, so it is sensible to dress accordingly.

I hope you will enjoy these walks into history and gain as much pleasure from them as I have had in devising them. Happy walking!

*John Wilks*

# WALK 1
# KNOWLTON RINGS – TEMPLE AND CHURCH FOR 4,000 YEARS

## Length: 3½ miles

*Knowlton Norman church inside the Neolithic earthen henge*

**HOW TO GET THERE:** Gussage All Saints, which is 10 miles north of Wiimborne Minster, can be found on a minor road between the A354 and the B3078.

**PARKING:** There is ample roadside parking in the village, but please park with consideration for residents.

**MAP:** OS Landranger 195 or OS Explorer 118 (GR 003106).

## INTRODUCTION

This short walk starts from the Drovers Inn at Gussage All Saints and takes you through pleasant farmland to visit the atmospheric ruin of Knowlton church, standing in the centre of a Neolithic earthworks. The walk, on tracks and quiet lanes, is flat and easy underfoot and route finding is simple.

## HISTORICAL BACKGROUND

At Knowlton a ruined church stands inside an earthen circle, visual demonstration of the way a site has been used by successive religions for 4,000 years.

By 2500 BC the people of the Late Neolithic (Stone Age) had highly developed religious beliefs. The nature of those beliefs, and the form the worship took, are unknown, but the monuments built for religious purposes survive today. Huge enclosures called henges were used for worship and for ceremony. These were round, open areas surrounded by high earthen walls. Four huge henges were built at Knowlton, and it seems likely that a community of holy men lived there to tend to the religious ceremonies.

Religious practice altered in the succeeding Bronze Age (2000–1000 BC). The dead were now being buried in round barrows, or tumuli, often on high places that dominated the landscape, tombs so solidly built that they still survive today. Many round barrows were constructed around Knowlton, and the henges continued to be used for ceremonies. Religious beliefs in the Bronze Age are shrouded in mystery, but those of the later Celtic inhabitants of Britain are better documented. They involved a complex form of nature worship, with many gods representing different aspects of the natural world. Worship was led by priests, called druids by the Roman invaders, and conducted in the open air, often at the old religious sites that had served this purpose for so long.

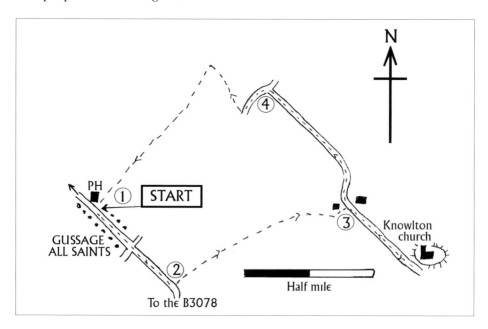

Although Britain was nominally Christian under the later Roman Empire, the old beliefs based upon nature worship continued. When St Augustine arrived in England in AD 597 he was determined to stamp out the old religions, and one way of doing this was to incorporate them into Christianity. The pagan feast of midwinter had become Christmas, and churches were often built inside the old henges, so that traditional sites of worship could now be pressed into the service of the latest god to arrive. It is believed a Saxon church was built inside the largest of the Knowlton henges.

When the Normans conquered England, they set about controlling the Saxon population with demonstrations of their wealth and power. Stone castles were built across the landscape, huge cathedrals were erected, and the simple wooden churches of the Saxons replaced by imposing stone Norman ones. The Norman church inside Knowlton henge was built in the 12th century and stands, although ruined, to this day.

## THE WALK

❶ With your back to the Drovers Inn, turn left and walk along the quiet village street to reach a crossroads. Here keep ahead, direction 'Bowerswain', and follow the lane downhill. At the bottom of the hill, just before the lane bears right over a bridge, turn left into a track.

❷ In 100 yards bear left into a green-hedged track, leaving the stream. Follow the track, soon narrowing to a footpath between hedgerows. At a T-junction, turn left. Keep on past a house and out to a lane in front of a farm.

❸ Turn right along the lane for ¼ mile to reach the ruined Knowlton church.

*Knowlton church stands inside the largest of four henges known as Knowlton Rings. The rings were constructed in 2500 BC, towards the end of the Neolithic period, when the centre of population had moved away from Cranborne Chase, 2 miles north. This, the largest henge, consists of an earthen bank with a ditch inside it, pierced by two entrances, one to the south-west and one opposite, to the north-east. There are three other smaller ring henges in the immediate vicinity, and also slight evidence of a ceremonial avenue, a pathway lined by earthen banks, leading to the complex.*

*One theory is that on special occasions the priesthood led a procession along the avenues and into the henge, and ceremonies would then take place in the centre. The bank around provided a grandstand from which the ordinary population could watch, while kept at a distance by the interior ditch.*

*Visible just to the east is the tree-shrouded bulk of the Great Barrow, the largest round barrow in Dorset. This is a burial mound, raised in the Bronze Age. Its proximity to the Knowlton Rings speaks of their continued use as a religious site.*

> **REFRESHMENTS**
>
> The Drovers Inn is a walker-friendly old pub, with oak beams and flagstone floors, offering a good range of food and local beers. It also has a large beer garden. Telephone: 01258 840084.

*There was a village here from Saxon times. The name Knowlton comes from the old English 'tun', or settlement, on the hill, or 'knoll'. Nothing remains of the Saxon church believed to have stood in this henge. The present church was built by the Normans in the early 12th century, and was remodelled in the 14th century, when the tower was added. There was a thriving village around the church until 1485, when the community was decimated by bubonic plague and the survivors moved away. The church itself continued to be used until 1747, when the roof collapsed. After that it was abandoned and gradually fell into the ruin seen today.*

After viewing the church and henge, retrace your steps back along the lane. Pass the farm and the track you came in on, and continue along the quiet lane for another ½ mile.

❹ At a T-junction turn left along the lane. In 200 yards, at a bend on the brow of the hill, turn right into a track. Go through a gate and follow the track for 350 yards, until it climbs slightly and bears left. On the bend, turn left into a tree-lined grassy track, passing between iron posts (old railway sleepers). A waymark post is in the hedgerow on the right. Follow the track down to the village street in Gussage All Saints, beside the Drovers Arms.

# WALK 2
# CERNE ABBAS AND THE GIANT – GODS AND WORSHIP IN ANCIENT BRITAIN

**Length: 4 miles**

*The Cerne Abbas Giant*

**HOW TO GET THERE:** The walk starts from the Kettle Bridge car park and picnic site at Cerne Abbas, which is on the A352, 7 miles north of Dorchester.

**PARKING:** The car park is on a minor road that enters the town from the north, and is clearly signposted from the A352. (Kettle Bridge is not to be confused with a viewpoint parking area, which is 200 yards before the car park.)

**MAP:** OS Landranger 194 or OS Explorer 117 (GR 663015).

## INTRODUCTION

This short walk starts on the outskirts of Cerne Abbas, passing the remains of Cerne Abbey before climbing around the famous Giant to reach the top of the Downs. You then return via the hamlet of Upcerne (Up Cerne on many maps) to a viewpoint where the Giant can be seen in all its glory. The route is on tracks and field paths and quiet country lanes. There is one gradual ascent, which can be slippery after rain.

## HISTORICAL BACKGROUND

There is considerable debate regarding the age and origins of the Cerne Abbas Giant. One popular claim is that it was carved by the Romans, and represents the demi-god Hercules. Alternatively, it is said to have originated in the Iron Age, used by people who lived on the nearby hilltop as a warning to intruders. As there is no written reference to the Giant before 1694, it has even been bizarrely claimed that it was carved in the 17th century and represents Oliver Cromwell. However, the most likely origin of the Cerne Abbas Giant is that it was created by the Ancient Britons some 2,000 years ago, and is contemporary with another great hill carving in southern England, the Long Man of Wilmington, in Sussex.

The so-called 'Ancient Britons' were part of a far-flung Celtic world that stretched from the Black Sea to Ireland. The enemies of the Celts, the Greeks and later the Romans, portrayed them as war-crazed, woad-painted barbarians, whose only interests were fighting and orgies. In reality, the Celts were an energetic race who created brilliant and vibrant art, poetry and music, and had complex and deeply thought-out religious beliefs. They lived in settled communities, often quite large towns, and produced sophisticated and ingenious metal tools. What the Celts did not have was a written language, and the image of them that has survived is the propaganda of their conquerors.

The Celts were a race of warrior-farmers, and the basis of Celtic life was the natural world. Their religion reflects this. They did not believe in one god but in a host of deities, many of whom reflected aspects of nature. One of the most important gods was Nodens, the god of fertility and healing. Offerings were made to Nodens to bless a marriage and to make the couple fertile. His help was sought to cure illness and to ward off plague and other catastrophes that could afflict a society with only rudimentary medicines. Celtic artists often portrayed Nodens as a naked man, gigantically proportioned, and surrounded by symbolic objects such as a hare and a club. Celtic religious art had many representations of their gods. Some, carved in wood or stone, were tiny and intricate. Others, carved in the land itself, were huge, and the largest can be seen here at Cerne.

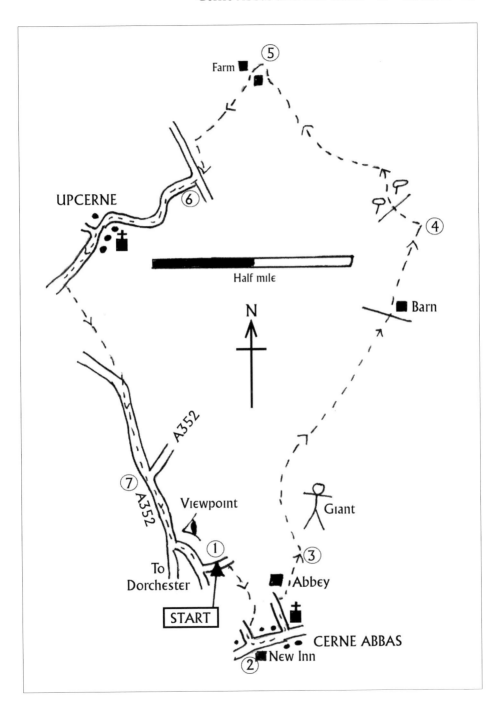

Farm

⑤

UPCERNE ⑥

✝

Half mile

N

Barn ④

A352

⑦ A352

Viewpoint

Giant

① ③

To Dorchester

Abbey

✝

START

CERNE ABBAS

New Inn ②

## THE WALK

❶ From the gates of the Kettle Bridge car park, turn left for 40 yards and then turn right at a finger-post, signed 'Village Centre'. Follow the riverside path into Cerne Abbas. DO NOT cross a footbridge after 200 yards but keep along the river, then along an enclosed footpath that soon widens to a lane. Follow it out to the main road in Cerne Abbas. Turn left for 20 yards to a T-junction in front of the New Inn.

❷ Turn left and continue along the main road towards the church. In front of the Royal Oak turn left and go up Abbey Street, passing the church on your right. Follow the road to the gates of the abbey.

*St Augustine, sent to England to convert it to the Roman style of Christianity, visited Cerne and preached to locals in the early 7th century. Nearly 400 years later, in AD 987, Cerne Abbey was founded by the Benedictine Order, 23 years after the same order had established nearby Milton Abbey (see walk 7). Although the abbey was pillaged and burned by Danish raiders within a few years of its foundation, it was soon rebuilt and flourished. Cerne was on the main road leading north from Weymouth, and a hospice, or hotel, was built to accommodate travellers, who often showed their appreciation with generous donations. The Abbey grew richer, and a new, imposing gatehouse was built in 1509, leading from the Abbot's house into the monastery proper.*

*Cerne Abbey was dissolved by order of Henry VIII in 1539. The buildings were bought by Lord Holles, who turned them into a private residence. But although the Abbey was gone, the town that had grown up around it flourished as an important staging post on the coach route from London to Dorchester and Weymouth. The monks of Cerne Abbey had laid the foundations for a brewing industry, and Cerne Abbas became famous for its beer. By the early 19th century the small town, with a population of only 1,500, nevertheless had 14 public houses.*

*Little remains of the abbey today. The imposing Abbot's House still stands, little changed on the outside, and is still a private home. The abbey porch and the hospice also remain. The churchyard of the parish church St Mary the Virgin covers the site of the monastic church, which consequently has not been excavated.*

*Cerne Abbas is a private house, but the abbey buildings are open to the public on occasions. There is a small entrance fee.*

To continue the walk, go through the gate to the right of the entrance to the abbey, and immediately go half-left along a path through the graveyard. Leave via a gate and keep ahead up the field (DO NOT turn right on a path that follows the wall). Cross a stile in the top corner of the field and keep ahead up steps.

❸ At the top of the steps go left with the path, to pass below the Giant.

*The Giant cannot be seen in any detail from below, with only glimpses of the chalk trenches that mark its outline being visible. You will get a fine view from the other side of the valley at the end of the walk. Given its huge size, and the convex shape of the hillside, one must wonder at the skill and ingenuity that went into creating a figure that is, as you will see, in perfect proportion.*

Continue along the side of the hill with the path, which eventually becomes an ascending grassy track. Follow the track through gorse, bearing left to meet a fence at the top of the ridge. Cross a stile and go half-left, towards a barn seen on the horizon, beside trees. At a cross-track in front of the barn, keep ahead, passing the barn on your right and walking with a hedge and trees on your left.

❹ At a finger-post in 400 yards, turn left over a stile, signed 'Minterne Parva'. Go half-right down the field to go through a gate at a second finger-post. Cross a track and keep ahead downhill, on a footpath through the trees. Follow the waymarked path, soon turning left through the hedgerow to a gate. Walk down the field towards a finger-post in the corner of the field at the bottom. Go into the next field and keep ahead down the side of the field, the hedge close on your left. Soon join a track and keep ahead.

❺ Follow the track to a cross-track at a finger-post. Turn left and follow the track through farm buildings. When it becomes a surfaced lane, follow this for 250 yards towards the main road (the A352) but, 20 yards *before* the main road, turn left at a finger-post signed 'Upcerne'. Follow the path through a strip of woodland, eventually turning right across the road and entering the lane opposite.

❻ Continue along this quiet lane for 450 yards to reach the hamlet of Upcerne. Pass a side road on your right and continue along the lane for another 200 yards.

*Look to your right for a good view of Upcerne Manor and adjacent church. This is a frequent arrangement in old-established village communities, where the manor house and church were built a very short walk apart, whilst the dwellings of the ordinary villagers were a discreet distance away from both.*

Where the hedge on the left ends, turn left at a finger-post. Go half-right down the field, aiming for a lane just visible in the distance, between two trees on the far side. Follow the footpath down to a white gate leading into the lane. (If the field is under crops, you may prefer to follow the left-hand boundary of the field, turning right with the boundary in the bottom corner and walking close to the lakes to reach the white gate.)

REFRESHMENTS

The New Inn at Cerne Abbas is a spacious old pub that offers a range of bar food and an à la carte menu in its restaurant. Telephone: 01300 341274.

*The series of lakes are artificial, created as fishponds by the owners of Upcerne Manor to provide recreational fishing for themselves and their guests, as well as a ready source of food.*

Go through the gate and keep ahead along the lane to reach the main road (A352).

❼ Turn right along the road for 200 yards, to reach a car park and viewing point at a junction with a lane, signed 'Village Centre'.

*The Cerne Abbas Giant can be best seen from here. The huge figure is 180 ft high and 150 ft wide, and was created by 5 ft wide trenches being cut to a depth of 2 to 3 ft, and then infilled with chalk rubble. The picture people usually see of the Giant is an aerial photograph, and from that angle the figure appears distorted. Seen from here, however, it is perfectly proportioned, and it was obviously designed to be viewed from across the valley. The features of the Giant and the positioning of his limbs closely reflect those of a small bronze figurine carved into a pan handle, which was found 12 miles away at Hod Hill.*

*On the hilltop above the Giant are the remains of Iron Age buildings surrounded by an earthen bank. It is suggested that this may have been a temple complex, contemporary with the giant figure below. This is, however, unproven.*

Go down the minor lane, signed 'Village Centre', for 200 yards, and then turn left back to the Kettle Bridge car park.

# MAIDEN CASTLE AND THE ROMAN INVASION, AD 43

**Length: 3 miles**

*The fortified west gate of Maiden Castle*

**HOW TO GET THERE:** The walk starts from Martinstown village hall/phone box. Martinstown is on the B3159, 2 miles south-west of Dorchester.

**PARKING:** There is ample parking in a lay-by opposite the village hall.

**MAP:** OS Landranger 194 or OS Explorer OL15 (GR 646889).

## INTRODUCTION

This short walk goes from the pretty village of Martinstown across fields to Maiden Castle, with excellent views of the countryside around, and of the castle and associated tumuli. It is easy underfoot, route finding is simple, and the walk allows ample time to visit Maiden Castle itself.

## HISTORICAL BACKGROUND

Just to the west of modern Dorchester is the vast Maiden Castle. Today it is a spectacular green hilltop, loved by walkers and kite-fliers, but 2,000 years ago it was the scene of one of the bloodiest moments in the Roman invasion of Britain.

By AD 40 Rome controlled the greatest empire the world had ever seen, stretching from the Rhine to Tunis, from the Egyptian desert to the North Sea. But just off the Empire's northern coast lay Britain, an island rich in natural resources, divided into a number of independent kingdoms. The Britons were closely related to the Gauls of France, and indeed many Gauls had fled to Britain when Rome had conquered their lands, and the Britons supplied aid and refuge to their continental cousins who continued to resist the Romans. The twin incentives of seizing a resource-rich country and 'suppressing terrorism' led to the Roman invasion of Britain in AD 43.

An invasion force consisting of four legions and accompanying support troops, 50,000 men in total and led by the Emperor Claudius himself, crossed the Channel into Kent. Initial resistance was rapidly overcome and within months the south-east corner of Britain, along a line roughly from Colchester in Essex through London to Chichester in Sussex, was under Roman control. To extend their control the Romans now divided this army into three expeditionary forces, each consisting of a legion and support troops. The 9th Legion thrust due north, to subdue East Anglia and Lincolnshire. The 20th Legion went north-west, into the Midlands. The third force, the crack 2nd 'Augustan' Legion, drove due west, into the lands of the Durotriges and the Catuvellauni, the strongest of the British tribes who still opposed Roman rule.

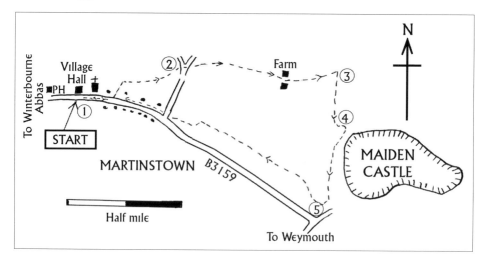

The 2nd Legion left the region of Chichester and marched rapidly along the line of the Hampshire and Dorset downs, elements of the Roman fleet sailing along the Channel parallel to them, to keep the troops supplied. The area of modern Southampton was taken, a quick thrust southwards seized the Isle of Wight, and the Solent was controlled as a safe harbour. The legion continued into Dorset, marching at a steady 20 miles a day. The Romans met stiff resistance all the way. Thirty battles were fought in open countryside, and 20 hill forts were taken, as the Durotriges and their allies fell back ever westwards. The Durotriges retreated as far as Maiden Castle, the mightiest hill fort in all Europe, and there they prepared to make their last stand.

## THE WALK

❶ From the lay-by, turn right and walk along the village street. Pass the church and 100 yards further on turn left up a lane at the side of Fishers Barn, at a finger-post signed 'Bridleway to Clandon'. In another 100 yards, turn right through a pedestrian gate and walk along the side of a field, the fence close on your right.

*Look half-right and you will see several huge mounds on the skyline. These are tumuli, burial mounds dating from the late Stone Age, 4,500 years ago, standing on Four Barrow Hill. Tumuli were raised on prominent hilltop positions, partly for religious reasons and partly to demonstrate that the lands around belonged to a specific tribe, whose dead watched over the land and were part of the community. The ridge to the south is lined with tumuli, a sign of how highly populated this area was from the Stone Age onwards.*

Go through a gate and keep ahead along the side of a second large field, to another gate.

❷ Leave the field and enter a lane. Turn right to a road junction, then cross half-left to a sandy track opposite, with a corrugated iron fence to its left. Follow the track, climbing steadily.

*Another tumulus is visible on your right.*

Follow the track through a farm, passing to the right of a large concrete barn. At the end of the barn turn right and then turn left in front of the farmhouse onto a concrete track, which goes around the farm buildings before resuming your original direction. Follow the track for ¼ mile to a gate.

❸ Go through the gate and immediately turn right onto a grassy track. Follow the track, Maiden Castle in front of you.

*Hill forts were built in the increasingly turbulent days of the Iron Age, partly as fortified administrative centres for the tribe and to provide emergency shelter for the farmers who lived all around, and partly to impress neighbouring tribes. The vast bulk of Maiden Castle covers the whole end of a natural spur, and is so huge it appears at first glance to be a natural feature. It was built by the Durotriges, the most powerful tribe in southern Britain, as a symbol of their power. Today the ramparts are grass-covered and have eroded into comparatively gentle slopes. When new, as high steep earthen banks topped by wooden palisades, they must have been truly awe-inspiring. The name comes from the Old English 'Mai Dun', meaning 'high hill'.*

Follow the track over the brow of the hill and then left down to a T-junction. To visit Maiden Castle, keep ahead through the gate and follow the path through the ramparts.

*You are going through the western of the two gates into Maiden Castle. This was immensely well fortified. A confusing maze of high and vertical earthen banks would have funnelled any attackers into a labyrinth of blind alleys from which there was no exit, whilst all the time defenders on top of the banks bombarded the attackers with missiles. The sling-shot was the projectile weapon of choice amongst the Gallic peoples of the Iron Age, and the Durotriges had a deadly skill with the weapon. The earth ramparts were topped with strong wooden palisades to shelter the defenders. At the inner end of the maze was a huge single wooden gate, blocking access into the fort's interior. Sheltered by the outer earthworks and only approachable on foot through narrow passageways, the gate was almost impregnable from attack.*

Once through the gate, bear right onto the top of the rampart.

*Maiden Castle was the largest hill fort in Europe. Three huge concentric rings surround it, each ring being a deep ditch, and behind those a steep earth bank, 20 ft high, would have been topped by a wooden palisade. The banks stretch for almost 2 miles, and enclose a flat interior that covers 47 acres (the equivalent of 50 football pitches). The hilltop site had been used since the Late Stone Age (3000 BC), when Neolithic man built a 'henge' here. This was an earth ring, approached by an earthen-walled causeway, used for religious purposes. Around 450 BC the Iron Age Durotriges tribe started to build the present fort, extending it over the next 150 years until it became the vast structure we see today.*

Turn right and walk around the ramparts.

*The interior of the fort was the cultural and administrative centre for the Durotriges. The king of the tribe had his simple palace here, surrounded by buildings that housed his personal bodyguard and his administrators. There would also have been the huts and workshops of weavers, potters, toolmakers and jewellers. The fort provided a centre for regular trade, both in imports and in goods manufactured locally, and merchants would also have had their homes and storerooms here. Much of the interior of the fort would have been a flat open area, suitable for providing emergency shelter in times of invasion for the farmers who lived on the plains below and for their cattle.*

Follow the ramparts to the eastern end of the fort, where a maze of earthworks mark the site of the eastern gate.

*This gate was similar in design to the western gate, but the defences were smaller. Whereas the western gate is on a level with the ridge that ends in Maiden Castle, the eastern gate stands where the ridge drops down to the plain, and the fort's builders thought the steep slope made such a massive gateway unnecessary at the east.*

*It was at this gate, rather than the stronger western gate, that the Romans chose to attack. It was a clash of two military cultures. On one side were the Durotriges, strong warriors skilled with the sling-shot and the spear. On the other side, the Roman legion, the mightiest military machine the world had ever seen. The Romans had siege artillery, huge catapults with which to destroy the wooden palisades that lined the banks, and ballistae – machines that fired massive arrows capable of piercing two men standing back-to-back. A strong force of archers and slingers also added to the barrage that was rained down upon the defenders. Under cover of this barrage the legion itself advanced, hardened soldiers who had spent years in training. The front rank linked shields, the next ranks held their shields above the heads of themselves and those in front, and the legion advanced like a huge metal armadillo against which the sling-shots of the Britons were useless. The Britons fought as individuals, the Romans as a unit, and discipline won.*

*Once the legion had forced its way up the ramparts and over the walls the fighting spilt out into the interior of the fort. The battle for Maiden Castle was ferocious. The British corpses included women and old men, showing that the whole population joined in the defence of the fort. The burnt foundations of huts have been excavated, speaking of the fort being burned after it was taken. With the fall of Maiden Castle, the resistance of the Durotriges was over. The 2nd Legion continued westward into Devon. They did not meet opposition on anything like the same scale again. Their commander, Vespasian, returned to Rome a hero, and became Emperor in AD 70.*

From the eastern gate continue around the ramparts, soon passing the stone remains of a building off to your left.

*These stones are the remains of a Roman temple, built in the 4th century.*
*After the 2nd Legion had taken Maiden Castle, they left a garrison in the area and founded the town of Dorchester, seen below. Maiden Castle was still used as a mercantile-cum-religious centre by the Britons.*

Follow the ramparts back to the western gate and return to the kissing-gate through which you entered.

❹ To continue the walk: from the T-junction, with the gate to Maiden Castle in front of you, turn right and go up the track, gorse on your right and the castle ramparts on your left. Follow the track over the skyline and down to a gate. Continue downhill on a grassy track, passing to the left of a large stand of gorse and following the track down a dry valley towards a gate onto a lane. Do not go through the gate, but instead turn right for 25 yards to a pedestrian gate into a field. (This is a permissive path, open until at least 2011.)

❺ Go through the gate and walk ahead along the field, keeping the fence close on your right. Follow the edge of this very long field for ½ mile, at which point ignore a gate going to the right but keep ahead along a second long field. At the end of the field turn left for 10 yards down to a gate. Go through the gate and resume your previous direction to a gate in front of a green-doored garage seen ahead. Keep ahead along the gravel drive to a lane. Go half-left over the lane to the grass verge beside a signpost. Walk along the grass verge back into Martinstown. Continue along the village street, past the church and back to the start. The Brewers Arms is another 200 yards further on along the street.

# WALK 4
# WAREHAM AND ALFRED THE GREAT, AD 890

**Length: 4½ or 5 miles**

*The defensive walls built by Alfred the Great at Wareham*

**HOW TO GET THERE:** The walk starts in the centre of Wareham, which is just off the main A351 Poole to Swanage road.

**PARKING:** In the central pay-and-display car park in Wareham, clearly signed to the east of the main street.

**MAP:** OS Landranger 195 or OS Explorer OL15 (GR 924875).

## INTRODUCTION

This pleasant walk starts in the historic town of Wareham, follows the attractive river Frome for fine views over Poole Harbour, then returns across meadows and tree-lined trackways. It ends up on the remarkably preserved 9th century town walls, which run halfway around Wareham. The walk is flat, and easy underfoot, although parts can be wet after rain. Route finding is simple.

## HISTORICAL BACKGROUND

The quiet market town of Wareham has a history going back a thousand years, when it was a key part of the defence of England against the Danes.

In the 9th century, England did not exist as a unified country, but was divided into a number of small kingdoms. One was Wessex, covering the area of modern Dorset, and parts of Devon, Hampshire and Berkshire. These kingdoms often fought one another as they strove for supremacy. But a greater threat to their security soon loomed, namely the Danes. Ever since AD 789 the Viking raiders from Norway and Denmark had attacked England, returning home with their plunder. But in AD 864 the pattern altered. For the first time, the Danes arriving in large numbers were not only fighting men but their families also, with the obvious intention not just to plunder England but to settle here.

The English kingdoms had no standing armies. Instead, they had the personal bodyguards of the king and his nobles, reinforced when required by the 'fryd', a militia of untrained and poorly armed peasants, mobilized

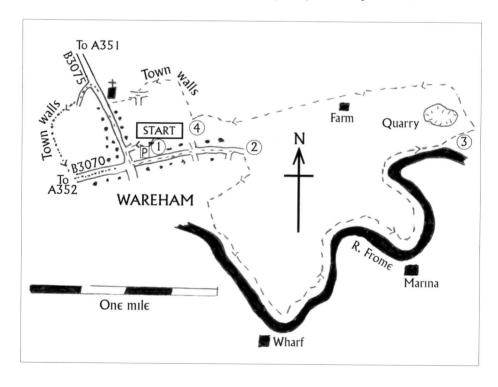

(very slowly) when needed and available to fight only when rural activities such as planting and harvesting permitted. This proved no match for the Danes. In seven short years, the small English kingdoms were conquered one by one, until by AD 871 only Wessex remained free from Danish control. In that year Ethelred, King of Wessex, died and was succeeded by his youngest brother, Alfred.

For eight years Alfred held the Danes at bay, in costly and inconclusive campaigns that were doomed to ultimately fail against the superior Danish forces. Alfred learned hard lessons during this period. He realized that the slowly gathered and poorly trained fryd was no match for the highly mobile Danes, whose standing army, with complete control of the sea, was able to strike at will anywhere in the kingdom and be gone before the English could organize a defence. To counter these advantages, Alfred set about a revolutionary overhaul of Wessex's defences. Firstly, he reorganised his army. The fryd was divided into two, one half always left at home to continue working the land, the other half available for prolonged campaigning as required. In addition, a third of the nobility, together with their professional bodyguards, were to be at the king's side at all times. In this way, the nucleus of a regular army was formed. Secondly, warships were built, to challenge the Danish supremacy at sea. And thirdly, numerous towns were strongly fortified, to provide ready shelter for the surrounding country folk in the event of a Danish raid and to provide a defensive stronghold that would delay the Danish advance until the royal army could arrive. One such fortified town, or 'burgh', was Wareham.

Alfred did not succeed in ridding England of the Danes, but he did mount such a successful defence that a peace was concluded. The army and the navy he built, and the burghs he founded, formed the basis of England's future defence. Alfred preserved England as an entity, creating the basis of the later nation, and for this he earned the title 'the Great', the only English monarch to be so called.

## THE WALK

❶ From the car park, walk past the public toilets and along Howards Lane to reach the main street of Wareham (North Street).

*Wareham was initially a Saxon fortification. The main communal unit in Saxon England was the self-contained village. Larger towns, with any type of market function, were rare. Although there was a town here before the encircling walls were built, it was very small and only occupied a tiny part of the total fortified area. Only after the walls had been built did Wareham start to grow. Its distinctive street plan, with four roads converging on a large central market square, was laid down 150 years later by the Normans. Wareham flourished as a market town throughout the Middle Ages, growing in an increasingly haphazard way as more and more houses, mainly built of wood, were crowded within the encircling town walls. In 1762 a fire swept through the town, destroying most of it. Wareham was rebuilt in the Georgian style, retaining the original street plan.*

Turn left and walk along to the crossroads in the town centre, and then turn left into East Street. Continue along East Street to pass through the town walls.

*Alfred the Great fortified Wareham by totally enclosing it within strong earthen walls. Within the walls were the palace of the local lord and the barracks of his bodyguard. Much of the rest of the area within the walls was open ground. At the first sign of the approach of the Danes, the alarm was sounded and the peasants from the surrounding countryside, together with their goods and livestock, would rapidly retreat inside the town walls. The lord and his retinue, reinforced by the peasantry (whose lack of military prowess was more than compensated for by the town's fortifications), could then easily defend the walls until Alfred's army could arrive. By AD 899, the end of Alfred's reign, no village in Wessex, or neighbouring Sussex and Surrey, was more than 20 miles from a fortified burgh. We return to the walls at the end of the walk.*

Keep ahead along Best Wall Road. Pass Best Wall Crescent on the right and 30 yards later turn right at a finger-post.

❷ Follow the green track for 50 yards to pass through a gate, and after 30 yards turn right through a metal pedestrian gate into an enclosed footpath. At the end of the footpath go through a gate and keep ahead, following the hedge on the right as it bends left, then right again. At a T-junction, by a finger-post, turn left and follow the clear path, wet after rain. Continue along a boardwalk to reach the river bank and turn left.

*The river Frome was used to transport clay and coal from Wareham to Poole, from whence they were exported to towns along much of the south coast. Trade goods came back up the river and Wareham had a flourishing town market. Eventually the Frome silted up, and Wareham declined as a trading centre. Today the river is used primarily for mooring pleasure yachts.*

Follow the path along the river Frome, river to your right and marshland to the left. In ½ mile turn left with the river, with wharfs and a marina on the opposite bank. Follow the embankment for another ½ mile, until opposite the Red Wharf Yacht Centre. Bear left again with the embankment and follow the river for another ½ mile to reach the wooden barriers of a sluice.

Cross the sluice and keep ahead along the river bank, ignoring a track going sharp left.

❸ One hundred yards further on, keep left with the footpath, while the river bends away right. Follow the path as it turns sharp left.

*There is a fine view of Poole Harbour across the reed beds to the right. Poole Harbour provided the location of the first test of Alfred's new navy.*

*The Danes were a seafaring people, and much of their military success was due to their ability to sail unhindered around the coastline of England and strike anywhere at will. To counter this advantage, Alfred set about creating a navy. Large ships were built, which were not modelled on either the Danish or Friesian vessels prevalent at the time but were something unique and of Alfred's own design. They were not required to be ocean going, but to provide effective fighting platforms for use in coastal waters. They were twice as long as Danish ships, powered by up to 60 oars and therefore faster, and with many more fighting men on board for ship-to-ship conflicts.*

*In AD 896, six Danish ships that had been raiding the Isle of Wight anchored in 'a huge natural harbour', almost certainly Poole Harbour. Alfred sent nine of his new warships to blockade the harbour mouth and stop the Danes from getting away. The ensuing battle was clumsy and inconclusive, with both sides running aground at various times. Nevertheless, two Danish ships were destroyed and 120 Danes slain, for the loss of 60 Saxons. Alfred had successfully demonstrated that the Danes could be challenged at sea, and thereafter the Danes were forced to be more cautious in their attacks upon the English coast.*

Pass a kissing-gate on your right, and follow a permissive path, soon fenced and with a flooded quarry to the left, to reach another kissing-gate.

*Clay quarrying has always been a major industry for Wareham. Clay from the Isle of Purbeck is especially suitable for working into pottery and has been used for this purpose since prehistoric times. Once the Industrial Revolution got underway in the late 18th century, the potteries of Staffordshire massively increased their production. This went well beyond the capacity of local sources of clay, and Portland clay was highly sought after. At its heyday, around 1820, 20,000 tons of clay a year were being shipped from Purbeck quarries via Poole Harbour to Liverpool and hence to the Potteries, and a third of all English pottery was made from Purbeck clay.*

Keep ahead across the salt meadow, with gorse and a hedge close on your left, and soon following the remains of a surfaced track. Maintain your direction through a line of trees and keep ahead along a track, more trees on the left, until you reach a kissing-gate on your left. Go through and then resume your previous direction along a tree-lined track, soon passing a farm on your left. Join a tarmac drive and maintain the same direction, soon crossing a quarry access road. Keep ahead along the

drive. Exit through the gates of Bestwall Park Nature Reserve and continue along the drive as it curves left, with a steep bank on the right. Fifty yards later, at a finger-post, turn left up the bank.

*The walls built by Alfred to surround Wareham were high, steep earthen mounds, rising 20 ft above the flat lands around. To the north and the south rivers provided a natural moat, while to the east the marshes adjoining Poole Harbour were another natural defence. Most of the land within the walls, to your left as you are walking, was initially a large open area, suitable for evacuees from the surrounding countryside, together with their livestock, to camp out on. After a thousand years, erosion has lowered the town walls and softened their gradient. They are still an imposing feature, and in Alfred's day must have appeared impregnable, especially to Danish raiders used to fighting in open countryside.*

❹ Turn right along the wall, following the path to reach a road. Maintain your direction for 20 yards, then turn left into another road, signed 'Walls Walk'. After 30 yards, turn right and follow the footpath to St Martin's church.

*St Martin's is Saxon in origin, with Norman additions. It is one of the oldest churches in Dorset. Within is an effigy of T.E. Lawrence (Lawrence of Arabia, see walk 14).*

Follow the path down from the church to the road. To return to the start of the walk, keep ahead along the road, soon to reach Howards Lane on your left, leading back to the car park.

However, it is well worth adding an extra ½ mile to the walk and following the town walls along their most imposing section. To do this, cross the road from the church and turn right. Go downhill for 80 yards, and then turn left up Shatters Hill. Follow the road for 150 yards, then bear right onto a footpath along the walls. Where the wall ends, descend to the road and turn left along West Street. Walk back to the crossroads in the middle of town, and then turn left for 100 yards. Howards Lane is on your right.

# WALK 5
# PARNHAM HOUSE – COUNTRY LIFE IN THE MIDDLE AGES

**Length: 6½ miles**

*St Mary's church, Netherbury*

**HOW TO GET THERE:** The walk starts from the Half Moon public house at Melplash. Melplash is on the A3066, 2 miles south of Beaminster and 4 miles north of Bridport.

**PARKING:** There is parking in a lay-by opposite the pub.

**MAP:** OS Landranger 193 or OS Explorer 117 (GR 485976).

## INTRODUCTION

This walk crosses pleasant farmland and goes through the pretty village of Netherbury before passing Parnham House and entering its deer park. You then climb a spectacular gorge to reach the top of South Warren Hill, where

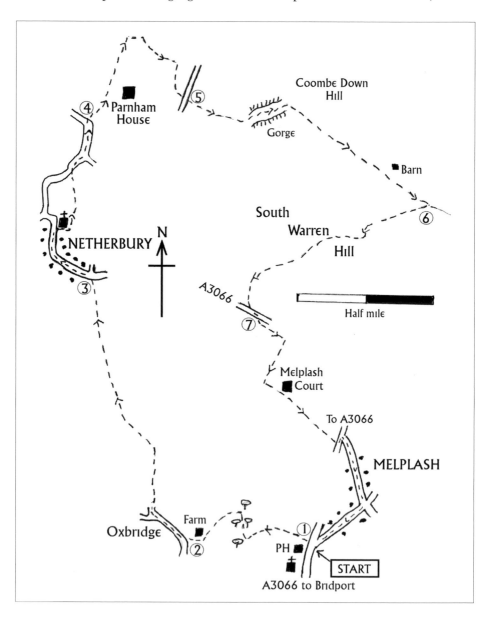

there are wonderful views. You return across farmland, passing another fine old house, Melplash Court. Much of the walk is on country tracks, with one very short section of busy road. There is one strenuous ascent and one easy descent.

## HISTORICAL BACKGROUND

Many locations in Dorset have been the setting for events of national importance. But the county also reflects national history on a more local level, as seen in the village of Netherbury and the grand house on Parnham estate.

In the 12th century the landscape of southern England was very different to what we see today. Much of the lowland was still covered in forest, with largely self-contained communities separated by large tracts of woodland. The steep chalk ridges were barriers to communication, and the roads were of very poor quality. The majority of the population worked on the land, and the valleys of Dorset were blessed with rich soil, sheltered locations and a good climate. Although most food was produced for local consumption, some specialist produce was traded. Dorset was ideal apple-growing country, and cider became a major export. For, although Dorset was remote from London, it was no backwater. The old Roman towns of Dorchester and Blandford Forum stood on the main road from the capital to the ports of Devon, and became centres of trade and commerce. Lyme Regis and Weymouth were important ports in their own right, and added to the flow of goods in and out of the county.

Industry, too, was growing. The chalk downland was ideal grazing land for sheep. The well-educated monks who lived in such establishments as Forde Abbey were the first to appreciate the commercial potential of a well organised woollen industry, and spinning and weaving became important cottage industries in many Dorset villages. Numerous small rural communities came to be dominated by this small-scale industrialisation. Before long laymen – small landowners and merchants – came to appreciate the possibilities, and entered the textile industry. Great fortunes were to be made from wool, and the wealth created was often invested in building works. Many great stately homes, magnificent churches and fine manor houses are the by-products of the woollen industry.

Local landowners had tremendous power in their own communities. Although feudal obligations gradually faded away throughout the Middle Ages, until by the end of the 15th century they had all but disappeared, the rural labourer still worked on the squire's land and deferred to his landlord socially and economically. Dorset estates were also acquired by rich men from outside the county, as country retreats, and often rivalries developed between the established 'squirearchy' and the newcomers.

## THE WALK

❶ Facing the Half Moon, walk along a tarmac track to the right of the pub. Where the tarmac ends, keep ahead along a grassy track. Go through a gate and then half-left across a field, a stile soon visible in the trees ahead. Cross the stile and keep ahead into trees, soon turning right with the path and walking along a strip of woodland. Turn left, following the path out of the woods. Keep ahead down the side of a field towards the farm ahead. At the end of the field cross a stile and immediately turn left. Some 10 yards later, turn right and go down an enclosed footpath, a high hedge on your right. Cross a stile and keep ahead to a second stile leading into an enclosed footpath. Follow the footpath left and down to a stile.

❷ Cross the stile, turn left to reach a lane and then turn right. Follow the lane for 350 yards, ignoring a footpath on the right and passing thatched cottages. Turn right along a concrete track, signed 'Bridleway Netherbury'. Follow the track past houses and into a field. Keep ahead, soon curving left to a gate seen on the far side of the field. In the next field bear left, converging with and then following the left-hand field boundary to a gate in the far left corner. Go through the gate and keep ahead along the track for 600 yards, passing houses and barns before reaching the road at Netherbury.

*Today Netherbury is a sleepy little village, well off the beaten track, but it was once an important centre of rural industry. Although its inhabitants, as in many other Dorset villages, had been employed as outworkers for the woollen industry, the village's main prosperity was based on apple growing. Netherbury was surrounded by orchards, and cider production was a major industry. At its peak, 100,000 gallons of cider were produced a year, to be exported via Beaminster across much of the county. Many fine country houses and thatched cottages in the village date back to the 17th century. But it was in the 18th and 19th centuries that Netherbury really prospered. The orchards declined, and hemp and flax became the major crops. These were turned into rope and sailcloth in a flourishing cottage industry that utilized local traditional skills. A subsidiary was the making of nets, which supplied Bridport's fishing fleet. At its height Netherbury was a bustling community of more than 3,000 people, which supported a dozen inns, many shops and other 'service' industries. Today only 300 people live in the village.*

❸ Turn left over the bridge and follow the road through the village of Netherbury and up to the church.

*St Mary's dates largely from the 14th and 15th centuries, a huge and imposing building that reflects the wealth of the village. It contains a 17th century pulpit and a fine alabaster monument to the More family, the local squires who lived in nearby Melplash Court and who dominated this part of Dorset. The church was altered and renovated in Victorian times.*

Just below the church turn right into a footpath at a finger-post and walk along the bottom of the churchyard and around the church, ignoring a side path down to the river. Keep ahead along an enclosed tree-lined footpath out to a field. Walk on along the right-hand edge of the field to enter a track. When you meet another track coming in from the left, keep ahead, turning right and then left and then climbing.

❹ Where the main track bends left, at a finger-post, keep ahead along a lesser track, soon with glimpses of Parnham House down to the right.

*The Parnham estate was given to the Gerard family in the 1190s, during the reign of Richard II. It was to be a country retreat, a base from which to engage in the noble pastime of hunting, and the first Parnham House was built on the estate in 1400 as a hunting lodge. The Gerards were newly arrived in this part of Dorset, and at first could not compete in wealth or influence with the Mores of Melplash Court, squires of the parish of Netherbury. However, in the 1440s (the exact date is unknown), the last male Gerard died and the estate passed to Richard Strode, in whose family it remained for the next 300 years. Under the Strodes the estate flourished. Judicial marriages to rich wives greatly increased the family fortunes, culminating in 1522 with the marriage of Sir Robert Strode (or Stroud as the family now spelled its name) to the daughter of Sir John Hody, Lord Chief Baron of the Exchequer to Henry VIII. This marriage brought with it a huge dowry, with which Sir Robert set about rebuilding Parnham House into the splendid mansion seen today. Sir Robert also established a deer park around the house, stocked it with a fine herd of imported deer and thus maintained the original use of the estate.*

*In 1776 Parnham House passed out of the Stroud family, and subsequent owners set about modifying and restoring the property. After the First World War it became a country club, then during the Second World War it was used first as an army hospital and later as a headquarters for the American army. After the war ended it became a psychiatric hospital. Today it is run by an Educational Trust to provide training facilities for craftsmen in the furniture-making industry.*

Follow the track to a gate. Go through the gate and keep ahead along a fenced track to go through a second gate into a field. Immediately turn right and follow the fence down to the field corner, then turn left, walking with the fence and river on your right to reach a footbridge. Cross over and enter the deer park of Parnham House. Follow the footpath to cross a drive and then go half-left, following poles to reach a second drive.

*Until the early Middle Ages much of England was covered with forest, home to herds of wild deer. The forests and the deer were the property of the King, however, and there were serious penalties for anyone taking the King's Deer without his permission. Parnham House started as a hunting lodge, where noblemen hunting in the Royal forest could find refreshment and sometimes overnight accommodation. By the 16th century, it had become common for landowners to create deer parks around their homes, where they could hunt their own deer without infringing upon Royal privilege. The present deer park was created in Tudor times and a herd of deer still roam the park.*

Maintain the same direction along a pole-lined path across the deer park. On the far side enter rhododendrons and turn right through a gate into a footpath. Follow it along the deer fence, then turn left to the road (A3066).

❺ Cross the road carefully, pass through wooden barriers, then turn right. Follow a footpath as it turns left around the boundary of an orchard. When you leave the orchard, keep ahead up an enclosed footpath. Cross over a field entrance and continue up the footpath, following it as it winds up though a spectacular tree-lined gorge. At the top of the gorge turn right on to an enclosed footpath, initially along the side of a track, then along the side of a field. At the end of the field join the track and maintain your direction, soon entering another field. Keep ahead along the side of the field, the fence on your right. At the end of the field, keep ahead along a track past a barn. After the barn maintain your direction along the side of a field, a fence on your left. At the end of the fence go through a gate and immediately turn right up an enclosed track.

❻ Follow the track (muddy in winter) until it turns left into a field. Do not enter the field but keep ahead along an enclosed footpath to a gate, then keep ahead along the side of a field. Follow the field boundary around to the right. Go through a gate in the field corner and then turn left to walk along the top of an impressive dry valley. Soon the path continues along a ridge, with spectacular views on both sides.

*This is South Warren Hill. In 1582, when plague struck this part of Dorset, the village of Mapperton, a mile to the east, was particularly hard hit and many people died. As Mapperton was part of the parish of Netherbury, St Mary's was its parish church and the villagers usually took their dead to be buried there. But the plague had not struck in Netherbury, and the people of that community refused to allow Mapperton's plague victims to be brought into their churchyard. Instead, they were buried here, on the summit of South Warren Hill.*

Pass through a gate and keep ahead along the ridge. Pass through a second gate and follow the path as it descends through trees and gorse. Enter a field and turn left, following the left-hand field boundary

**REFRESHMENTS**

The Half Moon public house is an old thatched pub, with a good range of beers and food. Telephone: 01308 488321.

downhill. Go through a gate in the field corner and onto a road (A3066). **BEWARE: although you are only on this road for 100 yards, it has blind corners and high verges, and traffic travels very fast along it. Take great care!**

❼ Turn left along the road for 100 yards, then turn right through a field-gate at a finger-post. Turn left along the side of the field, and in the field corner turn right to follow a tree-lined fence. In the far field corner cross a stile and turn left to follow a track around the outside of Melplash Court.

*Melplash Court was home to the More family, who have been landowners in this area since the Middle Ages. At the height of their power the Mores were squires of the parish of Netherbury which, in the 18th century, was one of the largest parishes in Dorset although it has since shrunk to less than half that size. The tomb of an unidentified member of the family can be seen in Netherbury church.*

Follow the track out to the main road (A3066). Turn left along the road for 30 yards, again taking great care, then turn right into a side road. Follow this quiet side road for 350 yards to a crossroads in Melplash. Turn right and follow the lane for another 350 yards back to the start of the walk.

# WALK 6
# FIDDLEFORD –
# THE MILLER'S TALE
### Length: 4 miles

*Sturminster Mill*

**HOW TO GET THERE:** The walk starts in Sturminster Newton, which is near the junction of the B3092 and the A357, 8 miles north-west of Blandford Forum and 7 miles south of Shaftesbury.

**PARKING:** Park in Sturminster Newton Mill car park and picnic area which is on the A357, 150 yards west of the town bridge leading into Sturminster Newton.

**MAP:** OS Landranger 194 or OS Explorer 129 (GR 781134).

## INTRODUCTION
This attractive walk is almost entirely over land once owned by the Abbey of Glastonbury. Starting in Sturminster Newton, by the 16th century water

mill, you walk through the town and over water meadows to Fiddleford, with its mill and manor house, and return through mature woods and fields. Walking is mainly on paths, with one short ascent.

## HISTORICAL BACKGROUND

In the Middle Ages one of the most important buildings in any community was the mill. Two can be seen on this walk through the Stour valley, at Sturminster Newton and at Fiddleford.

Until the end of the Middle Ages the majority of the population lived in small rural communities. Under the system of feudalism, most of the land in England belonged to a few influential people. The common people would have a small plot of land by their home on which to grow a few vegetables for themselves. But the bulk crops that made up most of their diet, cereals in particular, were grown in two or occasionally three huge open fields that surrounded each village. In these fields each villager held a number of strips of land, which he had to rent from his landlord, paying either in money or with a share of his produce, or by working for his lord for a certain number of days each year.

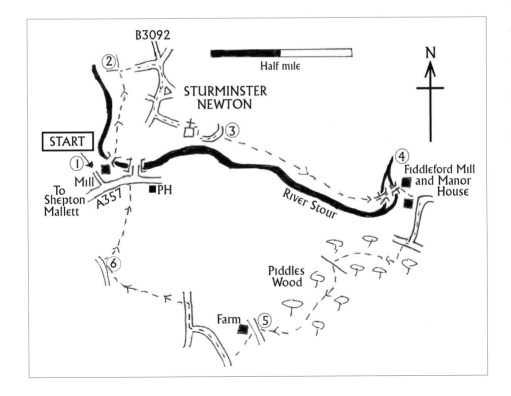

The most valuable tools and resources, such as ploughs or the teams of oxen needed to draw them, were beyond the means of the majority of villagers to own. Instead, they were owned by a few rich individuals, and rented out. But the most valuable and lucrative resource for any village was a mill, for even if villagers grew their own corn it still had to be ground into flour. The local landlord often owned the mill, which he leased to a miller in return for a percentage of the miller's takings. It was frequently written into the tenancy agreement of villagers that they had to use the landlord's mill, at non-negotiable prices.

The greatest landlord in feudal England was the Church, which owned 10% of the land and had 20% of the national annual income. The great monasteries held vast estates, scattered across the country, from which they drew rent. The Benedictines were the largest and richest of the monastic orders, founded initially to preserve and spread religious teaching but over the years becoming more and more wealthy and worldly. By the time of the Dissolution, many monasteries were deeply unpopular.

## THE WALK
❶ From the car park, walk down to the mill.

*Water power is the oldest form of motive power known to man. Water-driven mills were developed in the Middle East in the 5th century BC, and the idea was brought to Britain by the Romans. A water-driven mill has ground flour on this site since Saxon times. After the Norman Conquest, King William divided the Saxon lands between his followers, both secular lords and churchmen. Large areas of the Stour valley were given to the Benedictine Abbey of Glastonbury. Indeed, Sturminster means 'church lands' (minster) 'in the valley of the Stour' (stur). Sturminster Mill was one of ten that were spaced along the Stour valley, each serving its own community. Unfortunately, mills were normally made of wood, for cheapness and ease of construction. Unfortunately too, grain is highly combustible when it gets hot. Consequently, mills caught fire and burned down at regular intervals. The present mill, the last of a number that stood here, dates from the 16th century, and was built of stone and brick, which greatly increased its chances of survival. The mill was used continually until 1947. For a thousand years it ground flour. After the First World War this was no longer economic, and it was converted to produce animal feed. It ceased production in 1947, but in recent years has reopened on an occasional basis, and is now milling organic flour for human consumption.*

*Sturminster Mill is open to the public on occasions, when guided tours are given and milling is demonstrated. There is a small admission charge.*

Cross the bridges behind the mill to the water meadow opposite. Go through a kissing-gate at a three-way finger-post and then keep ahead along the river, in the direction of Colber Bridge, keeping the river Stour to your left. Follow the footpath to go through a kissing-gate beside a metal field gate in the far left corner of the meadow, and then keep ahead along the edge of a sports field to a finger-post on the far side. Go through a wooden kissing-gate and keep ahead on a footpath, the river down to your left. Drop down to the river level. At a four-way finger-post, turn right through a kissing-gate, signed 'Market Place'.

❷ Climb the path to a metal kissing-gate then turn left along a lane, ignoring side turns, to reach the main road (B3092). Turn right, passing the Swan Inn on your left. Keep right with the road, passing the small market square with the remains of the old market cross. Cross Ricketts Lane on the right and continue along Bridge Street. Opposite the fish and chip shop, turn left into Church Lane to reach St Mary's church. Keep ahead on the path, passing the church on your right, and then follow the path through the churchyard, passing the church hall and the old schoolhouse. At a T-junction turn right, and follow the path as it curves left and downhill to a lane. Keep ahead along the lane.

❸ Turn left with the lane and after 20 yards turn right, at the side of Ham Gate, into an enclosed track, signed 'Fiddleford Manor and Mill'. At the end of the track go through a kissing-gate and then bear quarter-right across the field, staying on a grassy track on the top of the bank, the river down to your right. Follow the track to a gate in the field corner. Cross a stile beside the gate and turn left along the left-hand field boundary. Pass into a water meadow and go half-right across the meadow, gradually moving away from the hedge on your left. Go diagonally across the meadow to a footbridge beside a finger-post in the far right-hand corner. Cross the footbridge and, after 50 yards, go over a second bridge. Cross the weir and keep ahead, following the footpath over the sluice gate. Continue with the path to reach the mill.

*This is another of the mills that lined the Stour valley, also ultimately owned by the Abbey of Glastonbury. Although Sturminster Mill is less than 2 miles upstream, so densely populated was the valley in the Middle Ages, and so important was milling, that another mill was located here. It was operated by a miller, who rented it from the local lord of the manor in the adjoining manor house. That lord in turn rented the mill and manor from Glastonbury Abbey.*

❹ Follow the path through the mill area and out to a lane. Turn right along the lane, to pass the entrance to Fiddleford Manor House.

*Fiddleford Manor*

The original manor house at Fiddleford was built in 1374 for William Latimer, who held the manor of Fiddleford as a tenant of the Abbots of Glastonbury, whose feudal land this was. As tenant-in-chief, Latimer collected rents and tithes from his neighbours. This included a tithe from the adjoining mill, and a proportion of the profits the mill generated. The manor house was a simple two-storey building, with service rooms on the ground floor and the living quarters, primarily a hall and a solar, on the first floor. A minstrel gallery was later added to the hall. The kitchen was a separate building.

After the Dissolution of the Monasteries, the lands of Glastonbury Abbey were seized by the Crown and sold off. Fiddleford Manor was bought by Thomas White in 1539. The days of feudal dues and tithes were long since past, and the mill was sold as a separate concern. White substantially enlarged the house during the next 15 years, extending the east wing and adding a new west wing. His initials, together with those of his wife Anne, can still be seen carved into the tops of the passage doorways. In the 17th and 18th centuries the house was enlarged again, which involved demolishing White's 16th century extensions. This new house was itself demolished in 1956, leaving Fiddleford Manor essentially in its original 14th century form. Its magnificent timber-ceilinged hall and minstrel gallery have been restored and are well worth seeing. Look too for the 14th century wall painting of the Annunciation in the upper hall, and the original glass in several of the windows.

Fiddleford Manor is open daily 10 am to 6 pm April to September, 10 am to 4pm October to March. Admission is free.

After viewing the Manor House, continue along the lane and follow it out to the main road (A357). Turn right along the road for 10 yards and then cross to a finger-post opposite. Follow the path up into woods. Climb the path, enjoying the bluebells and wood anemones in season, to a cross-track at the top of the slope.

*This ancient woodland has been used since prehistoric man first harvested its trees for tools and firewood. During the Middle Ages, the trees were coppiced, that is, the lesser stems were cut to produce poles from which to make fences and agricultural tools. The land was owned by Glastonbury Abbey, which took a tithe on all the wood that was coppiced.*

Turn right along the track to reach a cross-track at a finger post. Keep ahead, direction 'Broad Oak'. Ignore side paths and keep along the main path.

❺ Follow the path out through a parking area to a lane. Turn right along the lane for 5 yards, then turn left into a farmyard. Go between barns and keep ahead down the side of a field, the hedge close on your right. Walk into the next field and keep ahead to a gate opposite. Go through the gate and keep ahead past the side of a house to reach a lane. Turn right, follow the lane past houses out to a road and turn right again. Ignore a finger-post on the left in 50 yards, but after 100 yards turn left at a second finger-post (Hole House Lane). Go down the drive and into a field, then go half-right down the field, soon to walk alongside the hedge on your right. In the bottom corner of the field go through a gate and continue down a path through trees to a stream. Follow the path over a footbridge and up to a lane. Immediately turn sharp right into an enclosed footpath (Town Bridge).

❻ Follow the enclosed footpath to a stile on the left leading into a field. Cross the stile and then turn right along the side of the field, the hedge and fence close on your right. Follow the path and hedge, to go through a gate in the far right-hand corner. Go through a second gate after 20 yards and then maintain your direction, converging with the hedge on your right and following it to a kissing-gate in the field corner. Go down steps and then turn right, following the path out to a road. To visit the Bull Inn, turn right for 100 yards. To return to the start, cross the road at the traffic lights and turn left along the pavement for 150 yards.

# WALK 7
# MILTON ABBEY – THE LONG JOURNEY FROM MONASTERY TO SCHOOL

**Length: 3 miles**

*Milton Abbey*

**HOW TO GET THERE:** The walk starts from the church in the village of Milton Abbas, which is on a minor road 2 miles north of the A354 at Milborne St Andrew, and lies 6 miles south-west of Blandford Forum.

**PARKING:** There is ample roadside parking in the village, but please park with consideration for residents.

**MAP:** OS Landranger 194 or OS Explorer 117 (GR 806018).

## INTRODUCTION

This short walk starts in the quiet, picturesque village of Milton Abbas and visits the remains of Milton Abbey, with its huge and splendid mansion now incorporated into a private school. The walk then continues through woods and over fields back to Milton Abbas. The route is on tracks and paths, those through the school being permissive, with one ascent.

## HISTORICAL BACKGROUND

Milton Abbey was once a rich monastery. Today it is a private school. The journey from abbey to school is a result of the political necessities forced upon Henry VIII, which became known as the Dissolution of the Monasteries.

For most of the 15th century, England had been racked by the civil war later known as the Wars of the Roses, as powerful factions vied to control the crown. The reign of Henry's father, Henry VII, had seen several pretenders to the throne raising rebellion, and Henry VIII's own right to

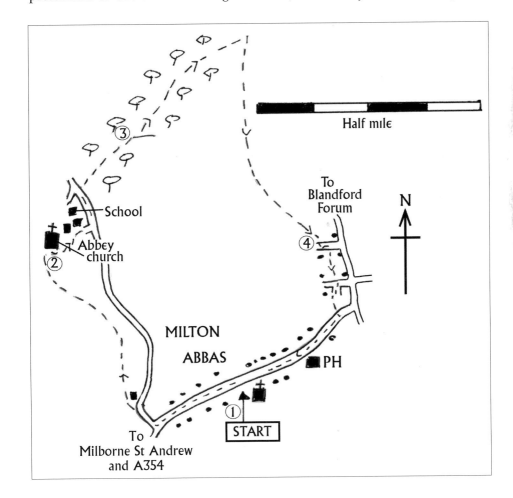

reign had been contested. Henry was desperate for an heir whose claim would be undisputed. This in reality meant a son, as it was doubted that a woman would be strong enough to rule. Many years of happy marriage had only given Henry one live child, a daughter Mary, and with no prospect of a son, the spectre of his dynasty being challenged after his death drove Henry to extreme measures. In 1527 he decided to divorce his beloved wife, Queen Catherine of Aragon, and marry the younger Anne Boleyn, who held out the prospect of producing a male child.

Unfortunately for the King, the Pope rejected Henry's ingenious arguments as to why his marriage to Catherine was illegal and refused to grant a divorce. To influence the Pope, Henry started to put pressure on the Church in England, increasingly curbing its powers and attacking its privileges. For five years the Pope resisted Henry's steadily increasing campaign against the Church, until in 1533 he finally excommunicated Henry. The King responded by declaring himself Supreme Head of the Church in England and the break with Rome was complete. Over the next five years the land and wealth of the Church was subject to widespread confiscation, and in the process known as the Dissolution of the Monasteries most religious houses were closed, their buildings demolished and their monks turned out to fend for themselves.

Milton Abbey, a religious building for 600 years, was sold to a rich Dorset landowner, Sir John Tregonwell, who used it as a farming estate. This was just the first step in a series of changes that culminated in the public school seen today.

## THE WALK
❶ With your back to St James' church, turn left and walk down the main street of Milton Abbas.

*Milton Abbey and the surrounding estate were bought in 1752 by Joseph and Caroline Damer, who set about converting it to a country house in keeping with their rising social status. The old abbey buildings formed the basis of the new mansion, whilst the surrounding grounds were turned into a formal park by the leading landscape gardener of the day, 'Capability' Brown. The only blot on the idealized landscape was the untidy village that had grown up around the abbey ruins. The solution was to build an entirely new village, out of sight in the next valley. You are now walking down the main street of that village. The neat houses, all built to a similar pattern, were originally dwellings for two families, one either side of a central hall, and were thus rather cramped. The steep-sided valley left no room for gardens, which had to be terraced into the valley side, very difficult to cultivate. The whole village was designed to be aesthetically pleasing rather than convenient to live in, but the villagers were given no choice but to move.*

At the end of the village turn right into a side road, signed 'Hilton'. Follow the road for 100 yards around a bend. Just before a thatched building turn left down a track (signed 'Milton Abbas church only'). The track soon becomes an enclosed footpath.

*To your left is the formal park designed by 'Capability' Brown in the 1770s. Central to it is the lake, artificially created by damming and straightening the stream that meandered untidily through the grounds.*

Follow the path to where it emerges in front of the abbey church, at a cross-track at a 'Keep to the footpath' sign. You are permitted to walk up to the church.

*Milton Abbey was founded in AD 964 by the Benedictines. Prior to the Norman Conquest virtually all monasteries in England belonged to the Benedictine Order, which was devoted to worship and prayer, and the preservation of Christian teaching by copying books and texts. The number and wealth of the Benedictine monasteries grew considerably after the Norman invasion, and they became increasingly worldly. Milton Abbey was largely destroyed by fire in 1309 and, although it was rebuilt on a grander scale, the church was never finished. The choir and transept were built, but the nave was not, leaving the imposing building you see today with a rather incomplete look. The wonderful interior was stripped back to its 14th century basics in the 1750s.*

*Although the incomplete church survived the Dissolution, most of the rest of the abbey buildings were demolished. The estates passed to Sir John Tregonwell, a wealthy landowner and the founder of Bournemouth. Tregonwell used Milton Abbey as the centre of a large farm. The surviving parts of the abbey buildings, mainly the abbot's house and guest lodgings, formed the basis of Tregonwell's farmhouse, which stood here for several centuries. The farmhouse was surrounded by farm buildings, around which in turn there grew up the homes of the farm labourers who worked the Milton Abbey estates. In 1752 the new owners, the Damers, set about totally rebuilding the house into a grand country mansion, the results of which you see today. The abbey is now a private school.*

*The church is part of Milton Abbas School, and a donation is requested for entering it.*

❷ To continue the walk: from the cross-track by the 'Keep to the footpath' sign, turn right and walk up the tarmac track, the small golf course on your left. (NB this is a permissive path, not a right of way, and the school reserves the right to close the path on occasions.) Follow the path past school toilets and outbuildings to a drive and turn right, signed 'No exit', though it only applies to vehicles. Follow the drive out to the lane and turn left down the lane for 150 yards, until you reach a drive coming in from the left (the rear entrance to the school). Opposite the drive, turn sharp right onto a track. Follow the track, a fence on your left and trees on your right, up through a horse-barrier.

**REFRESHMENTS**

The Hambro Arms in Milton Abbas is an old thatched coaching house, with a patio, and offers a range of bar snacks and restaurant meals. Telephone: 01258 880233.

There is also a shop and a tea-room in Milton Abbas.

❸ Ignore a track forking right steeply uphill, but instead bear left with the track, a field visible down to the left through trees. Curve right with the track and climb to reach a second horse-barrier at the top of the slope. Cross a cross-track and keep ahead through gates beside an abandoned lodge.

*These lodge gates stood on the boundary of the Milton Abbey estate in the 1750s, and were built by the Damers as part of the gentrification of their lands.*

After 20 yards, turn right at a bridleway sign into a field. Keep ahead along a clear track along the side of the field, a hedge and then a fence close on your right. At the brow of the field ignore a track to the left but keep ahead, the hedge on your right, towards houses. In the corner of the field go through a gap in the hedge and then go half-left across the next field to a gate leading onto a road.

❹ Turn left along the road for 30 yards and then, at the end of the recreation field, turn right into a waymarked, enclosed footpath. Follow the footpath out to a road. Go half-right across the road and turn down a side road. In 20 yards, at the end of the cul-de-sac, go right and then left again into an enclosed footpath. Follow the footpath as it winds down through trees to reach a road. Turn right along the road

*When the Damers built the new village of Milton Abbas, they incorporated an old coaching inn, the Dorchester Arms. This inn was renamed in 1852 by the new owner of the estate, Lord Hambro.*

Follow the road back to the start of the walk, passing the Hambro Arms.

# WALK 8
# SHERBORNE CASTLE AND SIR WALTER RALEIGH, 1590

**Length: 6 miles**

*Sherborne Castle, with Sherborne Old Castle across the lake*

**HOW TO GET THERE:** The walk starts from Sherborne railway station. Sherborne is on the A30, 6 miles east of Yeovil.

**PARKING:** There is a large pay-and-display car park in the town centre, a few minutes' walk from the station, otherwise there is roadside parking.

**MAPS:** OS Landranger 183 and 194 or OS Explorer 129 (GR 641162).

## INTRODUCTION

This walk starts in the historic town of Sherborne, which has many sites worthy of interest, and then goes through the ancient deer park, with excellent views of the two Sherborne castles. It returns through woods and along quiet country lanes, when there is the opportunity to visit the castles. The terrain is flat, and walking is mainly on tracks and lanes, good underfoot.

## HISTORICAL BACKGROUND

In the 16th century, Sherborne stood on the main road between London and Plymouth. Whilst he was travelling that road, the estate caught the eye of Sir Walter Raleigh, one of the giants of the Elizabethan Age. It was soon to become his home.

Walter Raleigh was born in Devon in 1552. Aged 17 he went to France and fought in the religious wars on the Huguenot (Protestant) side, before returning to Oxford where he studied law at Oriel College. In 1574 Raleigh was in London to complete his education in the Inns of Temple, as a lawyer but more importantly as a well-rounded Renaissance gentleman. To rise in the court of Elizabeth I one needed to come to the Queen's attention, and Raleigh's chance came in 1580, when he led troops to suppress a rebellion in Ireland. This gave him the opportunity to claim to be the court expert on Ireland, and he soon became the Queen's favourite.

Raleigh's half-brother was Sir Humphrey Gilbert, one of many firebrand sailors employed by the Queen to wage an unofficial 'cold war' against her enemy Spain. Gilbert had sailed to America in 1578, primarily to plunder Spanish ships and colonies, and had taken Raleigh with him. This trip had

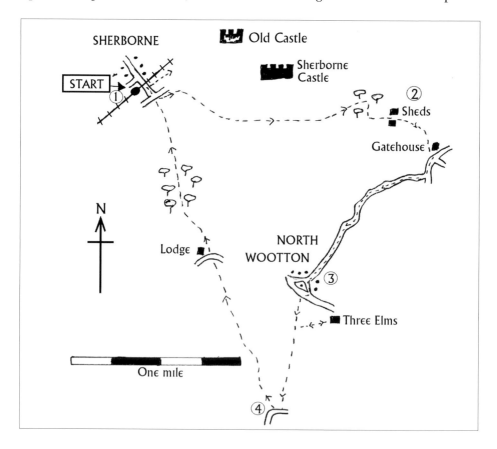

fired Raleigh's imagination, and he foresaw that it would be more profitable to found English colonies in America than to plunder Spanish ones. In 1585, now with the Queen's backing, he returned to America and founded a colony on Roanoke Island. Although the colony failed, it laid the first small basis of the British Empire. The Queen, pleased by his efforts, knighted Raleigh and gave him the Sherborne estates as a reward.

In 1592 Raleigh fell from favour. His secret marriage to Elizabeth Throckmorton deeply offended Queen Elizabeth, and Raleigh was sent to the Tower. Although he was soon released and again employed by the Queen to harass the Spanish, attacking their American colonies and Cadiz, Raleigh never regained the pre-eminent position he had had at court. In 1600 he was sent to America as Governor of the new English colony there, and did not return to England until 1603, just before the Queen died.

The new king, James I, deeply distrusted Raleigh, who was soon condemned for plotting against the new King and imprisoned in the Tower again, where he remained for 13 years. Raleigh was eventually released in 1616 to lead another expedition into Spanish America. When that expedition failed, King James had him executed in 1618.

## THE WALK

❶ With your back to the station, turn right along the front of the station and then turn right to cross the level crossing. Follow the road to a T-junction. Cross the main road to a two-way bridleway post and then turn left through a kissing-gate (ignore a tarmac path through gates on the right). Bear left on a gently rising grassy path, to reach a kissing-gate. (To visit Sherborne Castle, drop down left at this point to the entrance gate. Alternatively, the castle can be visited at the end of the walk.) Keep ahead on a clear path leading across a field.

*To your left is the magnificent Sherborne Castle. Beyond it, on the far side of the lake, the ruins of Sherborne Old Castle are visible. The 'old' castle was built between 1122 and 1139 by Roger de Caen, Bishop of Salisbury and Chancellor to Henry I. The Church held large tracks of land in northern Dorset, and leading churchmen were also secular landlords, charged with keeping the peace for the King. Roger built a fortified palace, both as an occasional residence and also as a base from which to control the surrounding countryside. Sherborne Castle was home to successive bishops until 1135, when it was seized by King Stephen during the long power struggle with his cousin Matilda. It was returned to the Church by King Edward III and remained Church property until passing once again to the Crown in the reign of Henry VIII.*

*Sir Walter Raleigh found that the task of refurbishing the now ruined castle and making it habitable was too great. Instead he decided to build a new mansion on the site of an existing hunting lodge. This four-storey rectangular building, called Sherborne Lodge, was completed in 1594. After Raleigh was disgraced and awaiting execution, James I sold the estate to Sir John Digby, Earl of Bristol, in 1617. Digby, while retaining the original lodge and keeping the face unaltered, added four wings to the building in the same architectural style. After the original castle was destroyed in the Civil War, the name 'Sherborne Castle' was applied to the new mansion, which stayed in the Digby family for another 200 years. The castle was further extended in 1787. In 1753 Robert Digby employed the pre-eminent landscape architect 'Capability' Brown to redesign the grounds, in line with the fashion of tidying up nature. Brown incorporated the ruins of the old castle into the gardens, and had the lake constructed between the two castles to provide a fairy-tale view. Sherborne Castle passed to the Wingfield-Digby line of the family in the mid 19th century. During the Second World War it was used as headquarters for the D-Day landings. The Wingfields still live in the castle today.*

Go through a kissing-gate and keep ahead along a sandy track, bearing left with the track. Where a green track bends off left, keep ahead through a gate and up the main track, climbing gently towards trees. Follow the track through a kissing-gate to a thatched lodge beside a deer gate.

*You are now leaving the extensive deer park that surrounded Sherborne Castle. It was this that first attracted Walter Raleigh to Sherborne, and he hunted here frequently.*

Climb with the track, on tarmac for a stretch, and then veer right through a deer gate. Continue along the track as it winds through woods, soon to pass green corrugated iron sheds.

❷  After passing the first shed, turn right along an access road. In 150 yards, at a cross-track, keep ahead and follow the track to a gatehouse and out onto a lane, where you turn right. Just before a telephone box turn right into a side lane. Follow this quiet country lane, with fine views over the surrounding countryside, for 1¼ miles, to reach the hamlet of North Wootton.

❸  At a T-junction turn left to reach the busy main road. Turn right along the main road for 10 yards and then turn left across the road into a track past a cottage.

*The Three Elms pub is just along the main road to the left. Alternatively, a short way down the track you are now on there is a signposted footpath on the left that also leads to the pub.*

**REFRESHMENTS**

The Three Elms pub in North Wootton is halfway along the route and offers an extensive food menu and a number of real ales. Telephone: 01935 812881.

There are also numerous pubs and tea-rooms in Sherborne.

At the end of the track go through a gate and keep ahead along the side of two fields to reach a lane. Turn right for a few yards. Where the lane bends left, keep ahead to reach an opening in the hedge in the corner.

❹ Turn right through the opening onto an enclosed footpath. Follow the pleasant woodland path to eventually cross a footbridge. Continue along the hedge-lined track for ½ mile to reach the main road. Turn left along the road for 20 yards, then cross to the gates of The Lodge. Keep ahead along a track, soon entering woods. At a cross-track keep ahead, following the track downhill and past buildings. On reaching a cream cottage, where the track bears right through gates, keep ahead to go through a kissing-gate. Go forward along the side of a rugby field/race track. Leave the field by a second kissing-gate and keep ahead, initially along an enclosed track and then along an enclosed foot-path. Follow the footpath as it drops down a wooded gorge to reach a road.

To visit the New Castle: turn right along the main road for 200 yards.

*The castle and gardens, which can be visited separately, are open to the public 1 April to 31 October (not Mondays or Fridays), 11 am to 4.30 pm. There is an admission charge.*

To visit the Old Castle: cross to a side road opposite (Gas House Hill) and follow this road back towards the station, but turn right through a kissing-gate just before the level crossing, follow the path across water meadows to a lane, turn left along the lane to a junction, and then turn right to the castle.

*During the Civil War, Sherborne Old Castle was held by Lord Digby for Charles I. It was besieged twice, the first time in 1642 at the start of the conflict, when the Parliamentarians were driven off. Digby held the castle for another three years, a constant threat to Parliamentarian supply routes between London and the West Country. In 1645 the Parliamentarians brought artillery from Portsmouth and captured the castle after a 15-day siege. After the Civil War the castle was further ruined, to prevent it ever being used again.*

*Sherborne Old Castle is open 1 April to 31 October daily, 10 am to 5 pm (4 pm in October). There is an admission charge; free to members of English Heritage.*

To return to the start of the walk, retrace your steps back to the station.

# WALK 9
# CORFE CASTLE AND
# THE ENGLISH CIVIL WAR

Length: 6 miles

*Corfe Castle*

**HOW TO GET THERE:** The walk starts from the gates to Corfe Castle. The town of Corfe Castle is on the A351 Wareham to Swanage road, and the castle itself is in the centre of the small town, just off the town square.

**PARKING:** There are two pay-and-display car parks in Corfe Castle, and other opportunities for parking within the town.

**MAP:** OS Landranger 195 or OS Explorer OL15 (GR 960821).

## INTRODUCTION

From Corfe Castle this walk takes you through fields, woods and shrubland before climbing up to the ridge of Brenscombe Hill. It then returns along the airy ridge, with magnificent views all around, to East Hill, a fine vantage point above the castle. The walk is on tracks and field paths, with one stretch of quiet country lane. There is one ascent and one steep descent down steps. Route finding is generally easy, but care needs to be taken across one stretch of farmland.

## HISTORICAL BACKGROUND

There has been a castle at Corfe for a thousand years, and in its heyday it was one of the mightiest fortresses in England. It has a rich history, which came to a sudden end in 1646, during the darkest days of the English Civil War.

The first castle at Corfe was built by Alfred the Great, part of the defences he put in place to halt the advance of the Danes. He built a simple but strong wooden-walled fort on a high hill that commands the only gap through the Purbeck ridge (in Anglo-Saxon, corfe means 'cutting'). Corfe Castle remained a royal castle throughout the rest of the Anglo-Saxon period; a later English king, Edward the Martyr, was murdered here on the orders of his stepmother to make way for her son, Ethelred (the Unready).

The strategic importance of Corfe was recognized at once by the Normans, and in the years immediately after the Conquest they set about

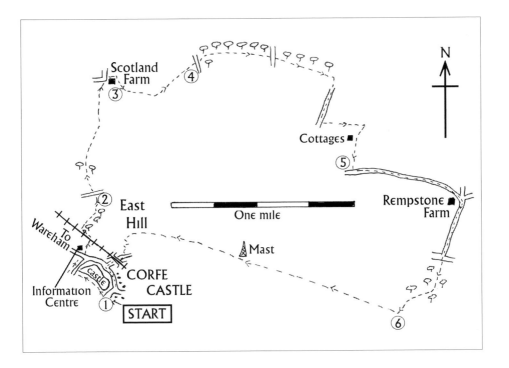

raising a stone castle in place of the wooden Saxon one. By 1106 Corfe Castle was a great fortress and state prison. It became a favourite residence of King John, who greatly improved its defences, work continued by his son Henry III.

In 1635 the castle was sold to Sir John Bankes. When the Civil War started in 1642 Bankes, an ardent Royalist, held the castle for the King, whilst most of the rest of Dorset supported Parliament. On May Day 1643 a detachment of Parliamentarian cavalry who tried to seize Corfe were easily repulsed, and they settled down for a series of blockades of the castle. Sir John was away fighting with the King's army, and it was left to his wife, Lady Mary, to command the garrison in the face of what, by 1645, had become a full-scale siege. With its commanding position, and well supplied with food and water, the castle appeared impregnable. But on 27 February 1646 a small force of Parliamentarian soldiers, posing as Royalist reinforcements, gained entry through the walls, opened the gates and allowed the main force to enter and seize the castle. In a spirit of chivalry, Lady Mary and the garrison were allowed to march out. In March 1646 orders were given for Corfe Castle to be 'slighted', and over the next few months the defences were systematically ruined. Corfe's days as a mighty fortress were over.

## THE WALK

❶ Make your way to the castle entrance. With your back to it, turn right past the National Trust tea-rooms and in 10 yards, turn right past a wooden barrier. Walk down a footpath under the castle walls out to a road.

*The ruinous state of the curtain wall above you is the result of the deliberate 'slighting' or destruction of the castle after it fell to Parliament in 1646. Explosives and undermining were used to ensure that the castle would never again pose a threat.*

Cross the road, go through two kissing-gates and over a footbridge, then curve right, up to a surfaced path.

*Below you are the ruins of a 13th century mill. It was owned by the castle and used to produce flour to serve the needs of the garrison. The mill was in use until 1790, when technological advances made it outdated.*

Follow the path along the millstream to reach the main road (A351).

*Look to your right as you walk along this path and you will see huge blocks of masonry, parts of the castle wall that fell here when it was blown up after the siege.*

Cross the road and pass to the right of the Castle Information Centre. Walk across the car park and up steps in the back right-hand corner. Go through a kissing-gate and after 10 yards turn right through a second kissing-gate and cross the railway, keeping a lookout for trains when crossing the tracks. On the far side turn left and walk, the railway on your left, to a kissing-gate in the far corner of the field. Follow the path as it undulates through trees to reach a cross-track. Here turn right.

*You are in the middle of disused clay workings, which were in operation from around 1750 until 1950. At this mine, clay was excavated in deep pits on the other side of the bridge behind you, winched to the surface in wagons, which were then dragged along a tramway, initially by horses, later by steam engines, to Poole Harbour. To your left are the foundations of a forge and stables, whilst to your right are spoil heaps of the unwanted soil that was excavated. The highly popular Portland clay was shipped from this and other Purbeck quarries to the Potteries, via Liverpool (see page 27).*

Follow the path as it winds through ferns, a fence on your left, to reach a road.

❷ Cross the road and climb steps to a stile. Maintain your direction across a field to a stile on the far side. Cross the stile and keep ahead through trees. On the far side of the wood cross a stile and go half-right across a large field, aiming for a stile into the woods on the far side. Cross the stile and then a footbridge, then turn left through a kissing-gate and follow the path through woods and across a clearing. On the far side of the clearing cross a stile and bear right, following a clear path through gorse to reach a road. Immediately turn right through the gate into Scotland Farm. Walk along the drive, and then onto a footpath to the right of a thatched barn. Go through a kissing-gate at the end of the barn, and then turn right around a corrugated iron dutch barn to go through a second kissing-gate.

❸ **Take care to follow the instructions carefully for the next five fields.** Go half-left across the first field, keeping a hedge and stream close on your left. Follow the hedge until 10 yards short of the bottom left-hand corner, then turn left through a gate. Keep ahead along the second long field, keeping parallel to the hedge on your right. Walk the full length of the field, ignoring an obvious gate in the hedge on your right, to pass through a gate on the far side of the field. (A waymark on the gatepost confirms that this is the correct gate.) Turn left and cross the third field to a gate leading into a fourth field. Go half-right across this field, aiming for two power line poles in the right-hand corner. Cross a footbridge beside the power line poles and then go half-left across the next, fifth, field to a stone culvert and a gate. Go through the gate and half-left for another 20 yards to cross a cattle grid onto a road.

❹ Go half-left across the road and through a gate at a cattle grid. Follow the track into woods, turning right after 100 yards. Ignore a turn to the left but keep straight on along a wooden track for ¼ mile to reach a road. Cross over and keep ahead along the tarmac bridleway opposite, following it around a right-hand corner to reach a lane. Keep ahead along the lane for 350 yards, then turn left onto an unmade track.

*You are walking along the course of the old tramway, used to transport clay from quarries at Corfe Castle to Poole Harbour, 2 miles in front of you.*

Follow the track for ¼ mile. Where the track turns left, with a metal horse-barrier in front of you, turn right through a metal gate. Go half-right across the corner of the field and drop down to a gate. Turn left along the track and follow it out to a lane.

❺ Turn left and follow the quiet lane, with pleasant views to both sides. In ½ mile, at a junction of roads, turn right with the main lane, passing Rempstone Farm barns on your right. Follow the lane for another 600 yards to reach a road. Walk across and pass through a white horse-barrier to go up the track opposite. In 200 yards, at a stone marker ('Corfe Castle 1¾') keep ahead up the main track. Pass through a gate and then immediately fork left up a side track. On emerging from shrubland, keep ahead to a stone marker on top of the Down.

❻ Turn right and follow the path along the ridge, with excellent views all around. At a telephone mast keep ahead along a permissive path. Follow the path along the top of the ridge, to reach East Hill, with magnificent views of Corfe Castle.

*The development of Corfe Castle can be clearly seen from this vantage point. The castle stands on a steep mound in the middle of the cutting through the Purbeck ridge. The original Saxon castle built by Alfred the Great stood on the highest part of the mound (to the right as you look at it). It consisted of a wooden tower, with a strong wooden palisade all around it, especially strengthened to the south (your left), the only place the slope is at all gentle. When the Normans arrived, they replaced the wooden tower with a great stone keep, and the palisade with a strong stone curtain wall. An additional, rectangular, tower was later added to the side of the keep.*

**REFRESHMENTS**

The Greyhound (telephone: 01929 480205) and the Bankes Arms (telephone: 01929 480206), the latter with a patio and beer garden, face one another across the small town square. Both offer a range of food.

There are also several tea-rooms in the town of Corfe Castle.

*In the early 13th century King John turned Corfe into a magnificent royal palace. He converted the interior of the keep, built a chapel and domestic buildings to the west (your right) of the keep and surrounded them with an additional curtain wall. He also added the curtain wall that surrounds the outer bailey (the large open space on the left slope as you look at it) and as an additional defence, dug the ditch that separates the inner and outer baileys. John's son, Henry III, completed the defences by adding the two gatehouses, one leading into the inner keep and one guarding the approach to the outer keep (on the extreme left as you look at it). Henry III also had the keep whitewashed in imitation of the White Tower of the Tower of London, which would have made Corfe gleam in the sunlight and visible for miles, an immediate reminder of the wealth and power of the King.*

*Corfe Castle is open daily all year round, from 10 am until 6 pm (April to September), 5 pm in March and October, 4 pm the rest of the year. There is an admission charge; free to members of the National Trust.*

Drop down the left flank of East Hill, towards the town, to a stone marker at the top of a flight of steps. Descend the steps to a lane and turn right under a railway bridge to reach the main road. Turn left, uphill, back to the main square and the castle where you started.

# WALK 10
# LYME REGIS – FROM PORT TO RESORT
### Length: 4½ miles

*Lyme Regis*

**HOW TO GET THERE:** The walk starts from the Cobb, on the harbour front in Lyme Regis, which is on the A3052 east of Seaton.

**PARKING:** There is a pay-and-display car park at the Cobb, and numerous other car parks in Lyme, as well as some street-side parking.

**MAP:** OS Landranger 193 or OS Explorer 116 (GR 338916).

## INTRODUCTION

The walk starts along the sea-front at Lyme Regis, before following the pleasant river Lim to Uplyme. You pass the impressive Carrington Viaduct, and climb over Horsemans Hill before descending the spectacular Ware Cliffs to return to Lyme. After leaving Lyme, the walk is mainly on footpaths and quiet lanes. There is one short and very steep ascent, and two descents down steps.

## HISTORICAL BACKGROUND

By 1750 Lyme Regis, a working port since Saxon times, was in serious decline, until it was rescued by the great growth industry of the late 18th century – tourism.

In AD 774 Cynewulf, King of Wessex, had given permission for a community of monks to settle at Lyme and extract salt from seawater. A town grew up around the monastic buildings, and a port was built to export the salt. By 1284 Lyme was sufficiently important for Edward I to grant it a charter, together with the right to use the suffix 'Regis'. There was no Royal Navy in those days, but instead, the king would hire private ships to fight on his behalf when required. Edward I used Lyme Regis as a base in his wars against the French, and hired local ships to transport his troops and fight when necessary. For the next three centuries, successive monarchs hired Lyme ships for their wars, and in 1588, five ships from Lyme fought against the Spanish Armada.

Lyme grew steadily in commercial importance, becoming a major entry port for goods in and out of Dorset and Devon, and its position as a

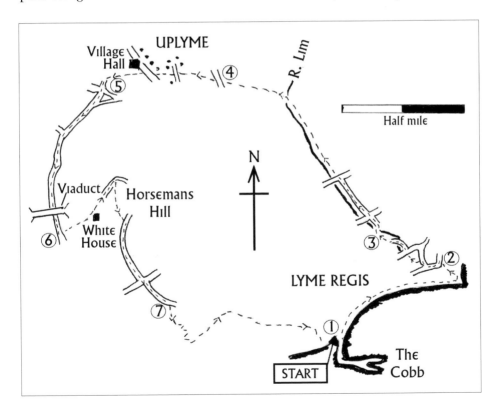

doorway to the South West gave it great strategic significance. It was used as a base from which to supply the Parliamentarian army during the Civil War, and was besieged by the Royalists. In 1685 James, Duke of Monmouth, landed at Lyme at the start of his ill-fated attempt to seize the throne from his uncle, James II. In the next century, ships regularly left Lyme to carry emigrants to the New World, and during the Napoleonic Wars Lyme was the major route connecting Britain with the Channel Islands.

However, Lyme has only a small natural harbour, even when enhanced by the construction of the artificial breakwater, the Cobb. This meant that it could only shelter relatively small vessels, and by the middle of the 18th century the port was declining in importance. Fortunately, a new trade was developing to boost the local economy: tourism. Sea-bathing was becoming increasingly popular, and from 1750 onwards there was a steady stream of visitors to Lyme. The town's popularity was ensured when it was described by Jane Austen in *Persuasion*, after the novelist stayed in the town in 1804. Throughout the 19th century tourists came to Lyme in increasing numbers, and although the town remained an active port, the harbour was increasingly devoted to fishing boats, used both commercially and for recreation. By the turn of the century, tourism was no longer confined to the affluent middle classes but was a mass industry, and with the arrival of the railway in 1903, Lyme's future as a tourist resort was assured.

## THE WALK

❶ To start the walk, stand at the Cobb.

*The Cobb was first built in the 13th century as a wooden breakwater, to provide shelter for vessels anchored in the otherwise exposed Lyme Bay. Over the centuries, it was added to, mainly in stone, but a bad storm in 1817 caused extensive damage. It was virtually rebuilt, using Portland stone from the nearby Isle of Purbeck, and extended in 1842 with the addition of the Victoria pier. There was a customs house behind the Cobb, and until the middle of the 19th century the major local products, blue lias (used to make underwater cement) and textiles, were exported through this harbour.*

With your back to the Cobb, turn right and walk along Marine Parade.

*The beach in front of Marine Parade was the centre of the 19th century vogue for sea-bathing, a recreation that was also supposed to have health-restoring properties. The beach was lined with bathing-machines, changing rooms on wheels that could be pushed down to the sea-edge to allow bathers to change their clothes and then enter the sea in privacy. A formal promenade was built along the top of the breach between the town and the Cobb. A 'library' was built on the promenade, a reading room-cum-refreshment room for the tourists. The building is still here today as Library Cottages.*

On reaching the Town Clock, keep ahead along the renovated harbour batteries to a viewpoint at the end.

*Across the bay in front of you is the distinctive peak of Golden Cap, at 617 ft Dorset's highest cliff. Here the rocks are laid down in horizontal bands, and erosion of the softer lower rocks has left a cap of the harder greensand, golden in colour and giving Golden Cap its strikingly flat top. The alternating bands of clays, limestones and sandstones give the cliffs along this stretch of the coast a huge variety of colours.*

With your back to the viewpoint ascend the ramp ahead, passing the back of the Mermaid Theatre, then keep ahead to drop back down to the main road.

*This descending alley, Long Entry, is all that is left of a road that ran from the centre of Lyme, climbing past the houses behind you, and then running along the clifftop that edges the sea to Charmouth, on the other side of the bay. These cliffs have been eroding for centuries, and by 1750 the road had fallen into the sea.*

❷ Turn left and walk down the road past the Tourist Information Centre, soon passing the Guildhall and Museum.

*The Guildhall was opened by Sir George Summers (or Somers), Mayor of Lyme Regis, in 1604. Lyme Regis was the starting point for many voyages of discovery to the New World, and Summers himself was the discoverer of Bermuda.*
*Next to the Guildhall is the town museum. Mary Anning was born in a house on this site in 1799 and devoted her life to the systematic study of fossils, classifying and categorizing the finds she discovered in Lyme Bay. Amongst them were the first complete skeleton of a plesiosaur, an aquatic dinosaur, and the first ever discovery of an ichthyosaur, the ancestor of modern fish. By the time Mary Anning died in 1847 she was recognized as a world authority on fossils, a remarkable achievement for a working class woman in the 19th century. Fossil hunting has been a major tourist attraction for Lyme Regis ever since. Fossils are the shells and skeletons of animals that died and fell to the bottom of shallow seas; over the millennia, the seas dried out and the sediments on the sea bottom became chalk, in which the animal remains have been preserved. Lyme Bay, in the middle of a long stretch of lias rocks that date from the Jurassic era (between 140 and 210 million years ago), is famous for the fossils readily discovered here. Although fossils had been known about for centuries, it was not until the early 19th century that they were studied scientifically.*

Turn right into Coombe Street and follow the road until you reach the Lyme Fish Bar. Turn left down the side of the Ship Inn, into Mill Lane. Keep ahead down the lane and along the alley to the side of the Town Mill, cross sluices and turn right along a path, the mill stream to your right and the river to your left.

*The mill stream is still used to power the town mill. Water is diverted from the river 200 yards upstream, (where this path rejoins the road) and as you walk along you will see the sluice gates that are used to drain excess water from the mill stream back into the river.*

At the end of the path cross the road and keep ahead up Mill Green opposite, passing to the right of the Angel Inn. Follow Mill Green as it curves left to rejoin the river.

❸ Bear right onto a footpath along the side of the river. Cross the river by a footbridge and continue along the road. At a crossroads keep ahead along Windsor Terrace, the river on your left.

*Note the 'Old Mill', now flats. The production of textiles, using the wool of sheep that grazed the Dorset downs, was a major industry in this part of the county in the 18th and early 19th centuries. The fast-flowing river Lim had a number of mills that powered the textile looms, the remains of several of which you will pass between here and Uplyme.*

Cross Colway Lane, the Horn Bridge on your left, and keep ahead along the drive. Where the drive bears right, keep ahead on a footpath, still following the river Lim. Cross a footbridge and enter a field by a pedestrian gate. Keep ahead across the field to a kissing-gate on the far side. Go through and cross a footbridge, then turn left, keeping the river close on your left.

*Note the remains of another old mill on your right.*

Climb with the path beside the mill and continue along an elevated tree-lined footpath. Join a track at a gate and turn left. Follow the track, eventually on tarmac, out to a lane in Uplyme.

❹ Cross the lane and enter a footpath, just to the right of a telegraph pole. Follow the broad path through woods, and then past the backs of houses, to reach a lane. Go half-left across the lane and through a kissing-gate. Follow the enclosed footpath to reach the car park of the Talbot Arms. Turn right along the road for 80 yards, then turn left into the car park of Uplyme village hall. Cross the front of the hall to a kissing-gate. Walk along the right-hand edge of the cricket pitch to another kissing-gate on the far side. Maintain your direction up the hill ahead, converging with trees on the skyline. Walk with the trees close on your right to cross a stile and keep ahead to reach a lane.

❺ Turn left down the lane to a crossroads. Keep ahead down the road opposite. In 50 yards, on joining another lane, bear right and follow the lane. In 350 yards, fork left with the lane, signed 'Shapwick 1'. Follow the lane for ½ mile to pass beneath Cannington Viaduct.

*By the middle of the 19th century the London & South-Western Railway Company operated between the capital and Exeter. The line was later extended further into the south-west peninsula, eventually to Plymouth, and down the valley of the river Axe to Axminster and Seaton. However, the high downs between the Axe and the coast at Lyme were a major obstacle to expansion in that direction. It was not until the rebirth of Lyme Regis as a mass tourist resort in the late 19th century that there was sufficient demand for a railway to make it economic to undertake the required engineering complexities. The Cannington Viaduct was built in 1903, to carry the railway across its last major obstacle en route into Lyme Regis, the steep valleys of the tributaries of the river Lim. The bridge is 206 ft long, and 93 ft tall at its highest. It is built of concrete, with brick facings, and was the first large-scale concrete structure to have been built in Britain.*

❻ Two hundred yards past the viaduct, just before a white building, turn left through a gate at a finger-post. Walk up the field and head for a gate in front of a white house seen ahead. Go through the gate and along an enclosed footpath to reach a lane. Follow the lane for ¼ mile, until it turns right at a red house. Just around the corner turn right up steps at a finger-post and follow the footpath up a steep wooded bank. Climb up the woodland path to a stile into a field. Keep ahead along the edge of the field, the hedge close on your left. Halfway along the field cross a stile on your left and then resume your previous direction, the hedge now on your right. At the end of the field, cross a stile and keep ahead to a field gate leading out to a lane. Maintain your direction along the lane for just over ½ mile to reach the main road (A3052). Cross the road with care and go along the lane opposite ('Ware ¼').

❼ Follow the lane for 350 yards, and then turn right into the drive for Ware Farm Manor. Immediately turn left over a stile at a finger-post. Follow the hedge on your right around a corner to a gap leading into a second field. Cross a stile and keep ahead, the hedge close on your left.

*During the Civil War, Lyme Regis had been staunchly Parliamentarian, and had even been besieged for a while by the Royalists. The Restoration of the Monarchy in 1660 was not popular, especially as it involved the suppression of the puritan form of worship. Dissenters, puritans who maintained their right to worship as they pleased, held open-air services on the clifftop here.*

**REFRESHMENTS**

The Cobb Arms at the start of the walk is a family-friendly pub that offers a choice of food all day. Telephone: 01297 443242.

There are also numerous other pubs, tea-rooms and restaurants in Lyme.

At the end of the field cross a stile and descend steps through woods.

*You are now descending Ware Cliffs, one of the finest examples of land slippage in Britain. A 100 ft-thick band of chalk sits on top of a band of greensand. Both are porous and allow rainwater to seep through until it reaches the underlying impervious clay. The clay itself slopes slightly down towards the sea, and becomes slippery, causing the waterlogged chalk and greensand to slide outwards after heavy rains, thereby exposing rocks that have lain underground for millennia. Ware Cliffs are the site of Mary Anning's most famous discovery, that of the skeleton of an ichthyosaur, which she found here in 1823.*

At the bottom of the steps cross a footbridge and 5 yards later, at a T-junction, turn left along a footpath. Follow the path as it winds down through the woods to reach a broad cross-track (the Coast Path). Turn left and follow the broad track for 400 yards. At a house, bear right onto a footpath, signed 'Lyme Regis'. Follow the footpath through a gate at a sign, 'NT Ware Cliffs'. Go under a natural wooden arch, and immediately turn right under a second arch onto the clifftop. Turn left along the cliff and follow the coast path, keeping right where choices occur. When a house comes into sight ahead, keep right and soon cross a stile on your right, signed 'Coast Path The Cobb'.

Descend steps through woodland, to emerge back at the Cobb.

*The open beach to the left of the Cobb is called Monmouth Beach, and is where the Duke of Monmouth landed in 1685. Monmouth camped in Lyme Regis for several days, drawing men to his cause, before marching northwards with the aim of seizing Bristol; 25 days and 25 miles later the rebellion came to an end at the Battle of Sedgemoor. Over 250 rebels were subsequently executed and twelve Lyme men who had supported Monmouth were hanged on this beach.*

## WALK 11
# EAST FLEET – HOME OF SMUGGLERS IN THE 18TH CENTURY
### Length: 4½ miles

*The Fleet provided secluded landings for smugglers*

**HOW TO GET THERE:** The walk starts from the telephone box at Langton Herring, which is just off a minor road, itself just off the B3157, 2 miles north of Weymouth. The telephone box is on the minor road as you approach the village.

**PARKING:** There is roadside parking on the road near the telephone box. The Elm Tree pub, in Langton Herring, allows walkers to park in the overflow car park, provided they are using the pub on their return.

**MAP:** OS Landranger 194 or OS Explorer OL15 (GR 615824).

## INTRODUCTION
This walk starts in the sleepy village of Langton Herring, and goes down to the Fleet, with fine views of nearby Chesil Beach. It follows the Fleet,

passing points with smuggling connections, including the famous Moonfleet Hotel, before returning on an inland route. The terrain is flat, on coastal paths, quiet lanes and tracks.

## HISTORICAL BACKGROUND

During the 18th century smuggling flourished around the coasts of England. The small community of East Fleet typifies that activity in Dorset.

Throughout the 17th century, successive governments had levied ever higher taxes to pay for foreign wars. To the long-established 'customs' duty, levied upon imports, was added the new 'excise' duty, a tax upon consumer goods and luxury items. All manner of goods were subject to taxation, such as wool, silks, tea and chocolate as well as tobacco and spirits. Evading

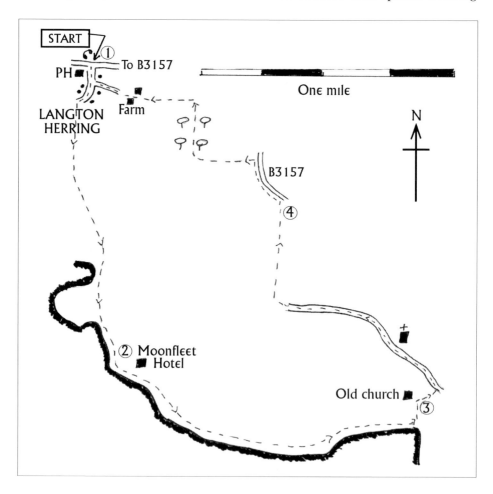

paying these taxes was viewed as a normal business operation, and customs officials were either bribed or intimidated not to look too closely. By the 1720s, however, the government was clamping down on such practices. Corruption was being weeded out of the Customs and Excise operation, and more men and resources were put into stopping smuggling.

Traditionally, many of England's seamen had used their skills in navigation to sneak a few illicit goods into the country, and as bribery and the open use of force were curtailed, smugglers turned more and more to discreetly landing contraband at night on deserted parts of the coastline. The Fleet, a quiet lagoon protected from the open sea by Chesil Beach and backed by sparsely populated countryside, was ideal for this purpose. The main commodities being smuggled were French wines and brandy, although there was also a flourishing trade in luxury goods like silks and spices, which 'fell off the back' of ships of the East India Company, en route to Weymouth.

Whole communities supported the smugglers, either actively (since smuggling was a lucrative source of extra employment) or tacitly (by looking the other way). Many local landowners were happy to buy duty-free brandy or silks, and in return to ignore the activities of the neighbours who supplied them. So important was smuggling to the local economy that whole communities would sometimes turn out to protect the smugglers. Smuggling flourished throughout the 18th century, until Britain's adoption of free trade in the 1840s made smuggling uneconomic as an activity.

## THE WALK

❶ With your back to the telephone box in Langton Herring, walk down the lane opposite, passing the Elm Tree pub. Keep ahead along a No Through Road. Turn right with the lane and 25 yards later, in front of Fleet Way Cottage, turn left into a track, signed 'Coast Path Moonfleet'. Follow the track through a gate and keep ahead. Chesil Beach is soon obvious in front of you.

*Chesil Beach is one of the more amazing coastal phenomena in Britain, a 16 mile long shingle spit that stretches from Abbotsbury, 3 miles north of here, to Portland Bill. Shingle is moved along the beach in a southerly direction, being picked up by waves and currents and deposited further down, and the whole beach is moving inland at the rate of 5 yards a century. It is up to 40 ft high in places. By a process not totally explained, the shingle becomes graded in size, with pebbles the size of peas at the northern end, and huge fist-sized stones at the south. This fact was of immense use to the smugglers who landed on the beach, for even in the darkest night an experienced smuggler could tell to within a hundred yards where exactly on the beach they were, simply by the size of the pebbles underfoot.*

After ¼ mile turn left with the track. Follow it for another ¼ mile. Then, 10 yards short of where the track enters a field, at a three-way finger-post, go right and immediately left to resume your previous direction, now with a wall close on the left. Follow the path along the edge of a field. On reaching water, turn left through the wall and continue on a clear path, the Fleet close on your right.

*The Fleet is a narrow tidal lagoon 8 miles long, cut off from the sea by Chesil Beach, which provides shelter from the worst of the winds and tides and creates a safe anchorage. The waters on the seaward side of the beach are, however, deep and treacherous, and many ships have been wrecked there, driven ashore by wind and tides. In the 17th century an attempt was made to drain the Fleet, to create arable land, but this was defeated by the nature of Chesil Beach. The stones of the beach are constantly in motion, and the effect of weather and the tides caused the water to percolate through and flood the land as fast as it was reclaimed.*

Go through a pedestrian gate and keep ahead. Follow the path around the headland to reach the Moonfleet Hotel, the crenellated building off to the left.

*What is today called the Moonfleet Hotel is built around an old manor house, Fleet House, that has stood on this site since the 17th century. This isolated old building, fronting onto the deserted and rather eerie lagoon, was the inspiration for 'Moonfleet House', the setting for John Meade Falkner's classic smuggling novel Moonfleet, written in 1898. (Fleet House was renamed Moonfleet after the novel became successful.)*

❷ Drop down with the path to a gate and go through a small wood. On the far side enter a field and resume your previous direction. Follow the path along the Fleet for another 1¼ miles.

*French brandy was loaded into barrels in the Channel Islands and transported across the sea by large smuggling luggers. These were met at night some distance off-shore by small fishing boats, which ferried the barrels to Chesil Beach, where they were rolled across and sunk in the Fleet until they could be moved inland at some convenient time.*

At the head of a bay, with a prominent barn on the skyline ahead and a walled house and church off to your left, go through a kissing-gate beside a field gate and turn left along a track, away from the Fleet. (A marker stone points to East Fleet.)

❸ Cross a footbridge and bear left with the track around the remains of a church.

*The small church of East Fleet also featured in Falkner's novel, as a hideaway for contraband. Unlike the use of Fleet House as the smugglers' headquarters, there is a factual basis behind this use of the church. The village of East Fleet had strong connections with smuggling; vaults beneath the church were used to hide smuggled goods, and there was even a secret tunnel that led from the vault to outside the churchyard.*

*The church and much of the village of East Fleet was destroyed by a tidal wave in 1824, when Chesil Beach was swamped by a gale-driven tide that lifted a 95 ton sloop, the Ebenezer, right over into the Fleet and sank two large merchant ships out beyond the shingle. Today all that remains of the church is a tiny chapel, which contains brasses commemorating the Mohun family, local landowners who dominated this area in the 18th and 19th centuries, and whose name led to the area being known as 'Moonfleet' (Mohun's Fleet).*

Go through a kissing-gate and keep ahead past a row of cottages to reach a lane. Turn left and after ¼ mile pass the new church on your right.

*This church was built in the mid-19th century to replace the destroyed East Fleet church.*

Keep ahead up the quiet lane. At a junction at the top of the rise, turn right with the track (signed 'West Fleet Holiday Camp'). In 50 yards fork right onto a concrete track. In a further 200 yards keep ahead along a cinder track. Follow the track out to a road (B3157).

❹ Turn left along an enclosed bridleway along the side of the road. In 100 yards bear right with the bridleway and continue, parallel to the road. In trees in a dip, turn left along a footpath. Follow the path along a strip of trees for 350 yards to enter a wood and after 100 yards, at a T-junction, turn right uphill. At the top of the slope, bear left with the track. Follow it for 400 yards then go through a farmyard, following the track past bungalows to reach a road at Langton Herring. Turn right and follow the road back to the Elm Tree and the start.

# WALK 12
# THE HARDY MONUMENT AND THE BATTLE OF TRAFALGAR, 1805

## Length: 4½ miles

*The Hardy Monument*

**HOW TO GET THERE:** The walk starts from the King's Arms public house in the village of Portesham which is on the B3157, 7 miles west of Weymouth. The pub is on the corner of the B3157 and Front Street, at a signpost for 'Dorchester'.

**PARKING:** There is ample roadside parking in the village, but please park with consideration for residents.

**MAP:** OS Landranger 194 or OS Explorer OL15 (GR 602856).

## INTRODUCTION

This spectacular walk starts in Portesham, and climbs through woods to the Hardy Monument, where there are splendid views all around. It then takes you along Bronkham Hill, with one of the greatest concentrations of tumuli in England, descends to the valley and climbs again onto a last ridge to return to Portesham. The route is along tracks and woodland paths, with two ascents, one of which is strenuous but can be avoided.

## HISTORICAL BACKGROUND

Above Portesham stands a monument to Thomas Hardy – not the author, but the local boy who went on to become an Admiral and who fought with Nelson at Trafalgar.

Thomas Masterman Hardy joined the Royal Navy in 1790. By then England was already effectively at war with France, a conflict that was to go on for another 25 years. Hardy, 21 years old, already had five years' experience in the merchant marine, and soon was promoted to lieutenant. It was as a lieutenant that he served on HMS *Minerve* in 1796, where his quiet courage and level-headedness brought him to the attention of his captain, the flamboyant Horatio Nelson. A deep friendship developed

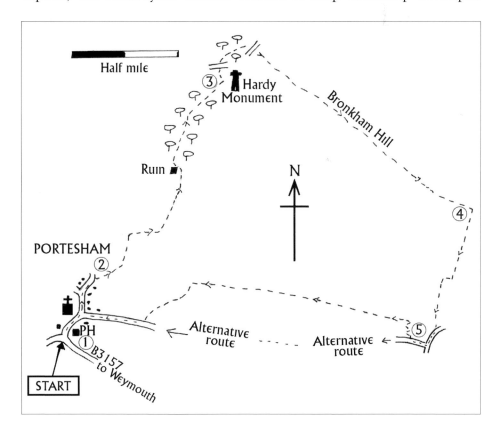

between the two men, and a professional relationship that lasted until the latter's death in 1805.

By 1805 the war had been going on, with one short break, for 16 years. France, now led by Napoleon Bonaparte, dominated most of Europe. Only England stood against Napoleon, who aimed to overwhelm his last remaining enemy, with a massive army, almost 200,000 strong, being gathered around Calais. Such an army would easily sweep aside the few troops and poorly trained militia in England, and the war would be over. For the invasion to succeed, Napoleon needed to control the English Channel for just 24 hours. Only the Royal Navy, outnumbered by Napoleon's fleet, stood in the way of total defeat.

It was of paramount importance to England that Napoleon's navy be destroyed, and after a summer of manoeuvres the English fleet, led by Nelson, finally succeeded in bringing the combined French and Spanish fleets to battle, off Cape Trafalgar in Spain. As his flagship, Nelson chose HMS *Victory*, commanded by his old friend, Thomas Hardy, now a captain. Nelson's plan was simple and daring. Traditionally, 18th century fleets lined their ships up one behind the other, sailed parallel to the enemy, and fired at each other, a technique almost guaranteed to result in a draw. Instead, Nelson divided his fleet into two columns, to sail directly at the enemy line and pierce it in numerous places, after which each ship was to engage in a furious mêlée with whatever enemy vessels it could reach.

The danger of this plan was that the leading ships of each column would be exposed to an ongoing broadside from the full enemy fleet for a full 15 minutes, until they were close enough to engage. Under Hardy's cool captaincy, the *Victory* led one column to smash through the enemy line. In the ensuing battle 17 enemy ships were captured at no loss to the English. The danger of invasion was averted and English mastery of the oceans was assured for the next century. But at the height of the battle, Nelson was shot by a sniper, and was carried below decks. Hardy, although busy commanding the *Victory* in the height of a fierce battle, was able to visit his mortally wounded friend several times, and it was in his arms that Nelson died, after uttering his last immortal words, 'Kiss me, Hardy.'

## THE WALK
❶ With your back to the King's Arms, look to your left across the B1357. On the opposite side of the road is Portesham House, home to Thomas Hardy.

*Thomas Masterman Hardy was born in 1769 at Kingston Russell House, 4 miles north-west of Portesham, home to the family that owned much of the countryside around. As the junior son of a lesser branch of the family, Thomas was raised here in Portesham House and, aged 12, ran away to sea. He was returned to continue his education at Portesham village school, but at 16 he again ran away, spending five years in a merchant ship before joining the Royal Navy in 1790. He remained in the Royal Navy for 30 years after the battle of Trafalgar, eventually being knighted and becoming Vice Admiral. Although Portesham House remained his home throughout his life, he spent most of his time at sea or in London. After he retired from active service in 1834, he took up the post of Governor of the Royal Naval Hospital in Greenwich. He died in 1839, and is buried in a mausoleum in its grounds. At his request, a miniature picture of Nelson was placed in his coffin.*

To start the walk, turn right and walk along Front Street, past the church. Pass a road to the right (signed 'Coryates') and keep ahead, soon bearing right with the main road.

❷ One hundred yards past the bend, turn right up an unmade track, signed 'Hardy Monument'. Follow it through a gate and keep ahead uphill, the track soon becoming grassy and tree-lined. Follow it as it curves right, a wall on the left. At the top of the field turn left and follow the track into the next field, soon curving right and keeping a wall on your right-hand side. Keep ahead into the next field, the wall still on your right, and descend to a gate leading into a track. Turn left along the track and descend. Pass through a gate by derelict buildings and then turn left in front of woods. After 20 yards, turn right at a finger-post onto a footpath leading into the woods. Follow this pleasant woodland path up through the trees, ignoring side turns and following signs for the Hardy Monument wherever a choice occurs.

❸ Emerge from the trees and keep ahead to the monument.

*The Hardy Monument stands on the highest point of Black Down, land owned by the Hardy family in Thomas's day and owned by descendants of the family still. In 1805 a beacon stood on this spot, one of many that was to be lit if a French invasion fleet was sighted. Napoleon's one chance of invading England was lost with the defeat of his navy at Trafalgar, although this was not fully appreciated at the time and fears of potential invasion persisted for a decade after. The monument was erected in 1844 by Hardy's daughters to commemorate their father and his part in the victory at Trafalgar. It is 72 ft high, and built of local Portland stone.*

*The monument is open at weekends from April until September, 11 am to 5 pm. There is a small admission charge; free to National Trust members.*

Walk down the entrance drive of the monument, then at a waymark post turn right down to the road. Cross the road to a finger-post and then follow the footpath down to a stile and cross into woods. Descend through the woods to cross a stile and follow the footpath out to the road. Turn left for 10 yards and then cross the road and go up a path at a finger-

**REFRESHMENTS**

The King's Arms in Portesham is an old pub with a large beer garden, and offers a good range of bar food. Telephone: 01305 871342.

post ('Inland Coast Path Osmington'). Go through a gate and keep ahead along Bronkham Hill, a wall on your right.

*The long ridge of Bronkham Hill is lined with dozens of tumuli, Neolithic burial sites, the greatest accumulation of such mounds in the British Isles.*

Follow the path to a gate. Ignore a footpath on the right to Hell Bottom, but go through the gate and keep ahead. Where the wall on your right ends keep ahead across the open downland, bracken on your left.

❹ Go through gorse and, immediately before a gate, turn right at a finger-post to 'Coryates ¾'. Cross a stile in 5 yards and then turn right on a track going downhill. Keep downhill, with a hedge on your right, to cross a stile in the field corner. Keep ahead for 20 yards, a fence on your left, then turn left through a gate. Follow the track gently downhill, a hedgerow on the left. Ignore a side turn but follow the track out to a lane. Turn right for 100 yards, then turn right into a side lane, signed 'Portesham'. Follow the lane for 150 yards and turn right over a stile up the bank.

❺ From the stile the path is undefined, and the right of way goes diagonally left up the slope. You need to reach the skyline and the best way is to zig-zag up the terraces until you reach the top of the slope. If this is too daunting, you can complete the walk by staying on the lane for a further mile. At the top of the slope turn left along the ridge to cross a stile. Keep ahead, the wall on your right.

Join a track and maintain your direction, the wall still on your right. Do not follow the track through a gate but maintain your direction, a fence now on your right. At the end of the fence, cross a stile beside a gate to the left of a telegraph pole. Keep ahead along the ridge, the fence still on your right. At the end of the field do not drop down the field, but cross a hurdle and then keep ahead, soon curving right to rejoin the wall. Maintain your direction along the wall to reach a gate in the far corner. Go through the gate and turn left down a farm track to reach the lane. Turn right along the lane for ¼ mile to a T-junction. Turn left back to the start.

# WALK 13
# TOLPUDDLE AND THE MARTYRS OF 1834

## Length: 4½ miles

*The village green in Tolpuddle where the martyrs met*

**HOW TO GET THERE:** The walk starts from the village green in the centre of Tolpuddle, which is on a minor road just south of the A35, 2 miles east of Puddletown.

**PARKING:** There is ample roadside parking, but please park with consideration for residents.

**MAP:** OS Landranger 194 or OS Explorer 117 (GR 792943).

## INTRODUCTION

This pleasant walk starts in the quiet village of Tolpuddle, and then heads out onto the Downs through open farmland with fine views all around. It returns via an Iron Age hill fort to Tolpuddle, where the story of the Tolpuddle Martyrs can be explored. The route is along good paths and tracks, and route finding is mainly easy, although care needs to be taken for one short section.

## HISTORICAL BACKGROUND

There was considerable political unrest in the air in the 1830s, and six men from the tiny village of Tolpuddle came to epitomize these times.

The spread of industrialization had altered the political fabric of England forever. The paternalism of earlier times was gone, and the structured social order in which everyone knew their place and by and large accepted that place was overturned. The labouring classes, both in the new towns and in the countryside, saw their economic lot worsening, with no improvement socially or politically. The 1832 Reform Act had extended the right to vote but had done nothing for the poor, whilst the Combination Acts of 1799 and 1800, passed to prevent unlawful gatherings by would-be rebels, were being used to effectively stop workers from organizing.

1829–30 had seen a wave of unrest in the countryside. In the face of bad harvests, landlords cut the wages they paid their workers. Bitterness at this

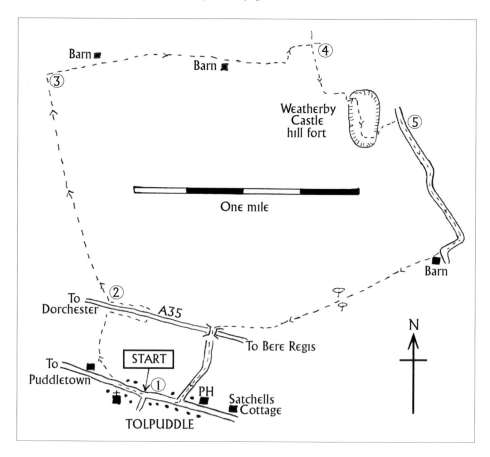

was combined with resentment at the erosion of the traditional rights of farm workers and at the loss of jobs caused by increased mechanization. Violence erupted. Under the generic name of 'Captain Swing', discontented farm labourers burnt haystacks, destroyed threshing machines, and threatened landlords seen as unsympathetic to the plight of the rural poor. The authorities retaliated and across England, 600 rioters were imprisoned, with 500 of them being transported to the colonies, and 19 executed.

By 1830 successive Enclosure Acts had effectively taken away any rights the agricultural labourer had to use a portion of the land he worked upon to grow his own food. He and his family were now totally dependent upon however much of a cash wage the landowner was prepared to pay. In 1833 wages paid to farm workers were cut once again, from 9 shillings to 7 shillings a week – the cost of supporting an average family was 13 shillings 9d a week. Such a wage cut thrust many families, particularly those with less than three wages coming in, to the brink of starvation. Many rural workers saw that only by combining together could their lot be improved, which the authorities, after several years of bitter unrest, were determined to stop. The quiet community of Tolpuddle was about to achieve national importance.

## THE WALK

❶ Start at the village green, on which stands the Martyrs Tree.

*A sycamore stood on the village green, and it was under this tree that George Loveless held a meeting, in October 1833, at which it was decided to set up some sort of union to fight against the wage cuts being introduced. Although Loveless was a farm labourer, he was an educated man with views seen as radical at the time. He was a Methodist lay-preacher and also a Chartist, a group devoted to parliamentary reform. This open air meeting was followed a few days later by a second meeting, in a nearby cottage. At this meeting the Friendly Society of Agricultural Workers was formed, all its members swearing an oath to support one another in their time of hardship.*

*The deliberations of this meeting were betrayed to the authorities. On 22 February 1834 posters were put up throughout Tolpuddle declaring that meetings and associations were illegal. Three days later, Loveless and five of his companions were arrested. The six men of Tolpuddle could not be tried for setting up a union, as this was not against the law. Instead, they were tried under the Mutinies Act of 1797, for 'swearing an illegal oath'. This law had been passed to stifle mutiny in the Navy and was obviously totally inappropriate in the circumstances of an industrial dispute, but it was the only charge that could be brought. The trial, held in nearby Dorchester, was rigged against the six from the start. Not only were the charges spurious, but the presiding magistrate, James Frampton, was a powerful local landlord. Several of his tenants were on the jury.*

*The foreman of the jury was William Ponsonby, who was not only the local MP but was brother-in-law to the Home Secretary, Lord Melbourne. The outcome of the trial was hardly surprising and the six were condemned to seven years' transportation, to be served in the penal colonies of Australia.*

*The original sycamore tree has long since perished, but the present tree was planted on the same spot to replace it.*

With your back to the village green, turn left along the main street and 100 yards past the church, turn right at a finger-post (signed 'Bridleway to Dewlish').

*The small Tolpuddle Martyrs Museum is 100 yards further on along the road. It contains a concise and very informative display about the martyrs and is well worth a visit. Admission is free. Telephone: 01305 848237.*

Follow the track past the backs of houses to a gate. Continue ahead on a footpath to the right of the gate. Gently climb with the path, through trees, eventually turning right with the path to a gate. Keep ahead on a tarmac track, the busy A35 on your left. At a T-junction turn left on a farm track and pass under the road. Immediately beyond the tunnel turn left up a track, the A35 now on your left again.

❷ At the end of the tarmac track, turn right on a clear path across a large field, aiming for a gateway in the hedge on the far side of the field, in line with the end of a wood seen on the skyline.

*Today the countryside around Tolpuddle is divided into large fields, owned by a few farms, but in the late 18th century it would have looked very different. Although the land was owned by a small number of big landlords, it was rented out to numerous tenant farmers, who either worked the land unaided or employed local labourers to help them. From time immemorial these labourers had had a stake in the land they worked. Even though most of their effort went into working for their landlord, they had tacit rights to a roof over their head, to a small plot of land on which to grow vegetables, to the use of common land on which to graze livestock. In times of bad harvest or individual distress, the parish or the local landowner would provide help.*

Go through the gateway and keep ahead up the next field, the hedge on your right. Pass into the next field and continue, hedge still on your right. At the far end of this second field, keep ahead along an enclosed footpath. Follow the footpath, initially downhill, for ¼ mile, to reach a waymark post. Here turn right.

❸ Walk along the bottom of two fields, the hedge close on your left, passing a dilapidated barn. At the end of the second field go left, and then right through a gate, then resume your previous direction along a grassy track. Pass through a pedestrian gate and keep ahead along a track. Follow it past a barn, through a field gate and then along the edge of the next field, the hedge now on your left. Leave the track by a pedestrian gate. Keep ahead along the edge of the next field to join a track. Follow the track through a gate to a junction of tracks and a footpath.

❹ Turn right over a waymarked stile and walk along the side of the field, the hedge on your left. At the end of the field cross a stile and immediately turn left to cross a second stile beside a gate. Keep ahead up the side of the field towards the wooded hill fort on the skyline. Near the top of the slope, at a waymark post, turn right and follow a faint track for 20 yards to the outer ramparts of the fort. At another waymark post on the first rise, turn left and climb up the outer rampart, soon swinging right to pass through the inner rampart into the centre of the fort.

*Weatherby Castle is an Iron Age hill fort, dating from about the 3rd century BC and built by the Durotriges, the same tribe that built the massive Maiden Castle (see walk 3). Weatherby Castle consisted of two high earthen ramparts, with a deep ditch between them, the ramparts topped by wooden palisades. There was one gate into the fort, a narrow, easily defended defile that worked its way between the ramparts and into the central area. It is this gate that you are now going through, although thanks to two millennia of erosion little of its original structure can be made out. Hill forts were built to provide shelter in times of emergency. There is no evidence Weatherby Castle was ever used in this way, and after the fall of Maiden Castle to the Romans in AD 43 it was abandoned.*

Keep ahead to reach the obelisk.

*The obelisk was erected in 1761 to Edmund Morton Pleydell, owner of Manor Farm a mile or so to the north. The Pleydells were landowners in this part of Dorset for generations, with strong connections socially and through marriage with the other landowning families of the area. They had originally been tenants of the Framptons, and a descendant of the latter family presided over the trial of the Tolpuddle Martyrs. What purpose, if any, the obelisk served beyond self-glorification is unknown.*

Route finding for the next short section is complex, so follow the instructions carefully. From the obelisk continue along an initially clear track through the centre of the fort. The track peters out and the way ahead is not obvious, but bear diagonally right to find a clear exit through the ramparts on the far side of the fort. Go through the outer rampart, cross the 'ditch' and go ahead for 10 yards through a line of trees to reach a

**REFRESHMENTS**

The Martyrs Inn at Tolpuddle offers lunches, dinners and also coffee and tea. Telephone: 01305 848249.

grassy sward between the inner and outer ramparts. Turn left along the grassy sward. Where the ramparts and sward curve left, look for a sandy opening going right down through the outer rampart. Drop down the track for 10 yards, then leave the track and bear left through bushes, slightly downhill. Soon a track and waymark post come into sight. From here route finding is easy again. Continue downhill to a stile leading onto a lane.

❺ Turn right along the lane for ½ mile. Turn sharp right with the lane and, 150 yards later, where the lane turns sharp left, keep ahead to go through a gate in front of a barn. Pass to the right of the barn and keep ahead up a grassy track. At the end of the track go through a gate and maintain your direction along a field, the hedge close on your right. Walk through a stand of trees to a gate and then keep ahead down a large field, the hedge close on your left. Continue, hedge still on your left, up a second field to reach a surfaced track. Go along the track, the A35 on your left, to reach a farm track. Turn left over a bridge and follow the lane back to the main street of Tolpuddle. Turn left for a few yards to reach the Martyrs Inn.

*A little beyond the inn, the White Cottage (no 55) was the home of Thomas Satchell. It was in this cottage that the Friendly Society of Agricultural Workers was founded and their fateful oath was sworn.*

*A little further on again is the Methodist chapel. In the early 19th century, Methodism was seen as a very radical movement, challenging the traditional Anglican Church and the established order that it represented. George Loveless was a lay-preacher at this chapel, and most of the other martyrs were chapel members. After the Tolpuddle Martyrs were convicted in 1834, there was a mass protest against their treatment. Sermons decrying the unfairness of the trial and sentences were preached in many Methodist chapels throughout England, this one included, and a petition with over 200,000 signatures was collected demanding their release. They were eventually pardoned in 1836, but due to bureaucratic delays the last of the six did not return to England until 1838.*

To finish the walk, turn right once you reach the main road and return to the village green.

# WALK 14
# CLOUDS HILL – THE LIFE AND DEATH OF LAWRENCE OF ARABIA
## Length: 4 miles

*T.E. Lawrence's cottage at Clouds Hill*

**HOW TO GET THERE**: The walk starts from a lay-by, ½ mile south of Clouds Hill Cottage on the road to Bovington Camp. Clouds Hill is 3 miles south of Bere Regis, and is clearly signposted either from the B3390 or from the Bere Regis to Wool road.

**PARKING:** In the lay-by.

**MAP:** OS Landranger 194 or OS Explorer OL15 (GR 825905).

## INTRODUCTION

This pleasant walk starts near the spot where T.E. Lawrence met with his fatal accident, passes his home, Clouds Hill, and then goes through Moreton Forest, crossing the river Frome to the tiny hamlet of Moreton, and the church where Lawrence is buried. You return through forest and over heathland. The walk is mainly on tracks, with one short section of road. Going is easy underfoot.

## HISTORICAL BACKGROUND

The wooded area of central Dorset around Bovington Camp, with the tiny village of Moreton and the isolated cottage of Clouds Hill, will always be associated with one of Britain's most enigmatic heroes, T.E. Lawrence, known as Lawrence of Arabia.

Thomas Edward Lawrence was born in South Wales in 1888, but from the age of eight lived in Oxford, where he studied modern history at Jesus College. In 1909 he undertook a walking tour of what is today Syria and Palestine, working as an archaeologist and collecting material for a thesis on Crusader castles. This area was then part of the Ottoman (Turkish) Empire, and during his 1,100 mile walk Lawrence, as well as becoming fluent in Arabic, fell in love with the Arab people and culture, and identified with their struggle for freedom from their Turkish masters.

When the First World War started, the Ottoman Empire allied itself with Germany. Lawrence joined Military Intelligence and was posted to Cairo, where he was soon taking an active role in leading the Arab Revolt. A charismatic personality with a great grasp of guerrilla warfare, he united the Arab tribes, captured the vital port of Akaba in 1917 and then went on to lead the Arabs into Damascus in 1918. Lawrence believed he had been

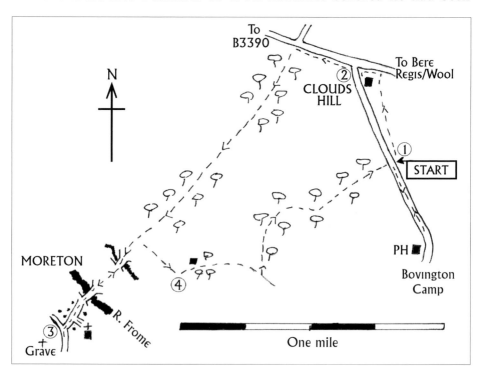

empowered to promise the Arabs an independent country in Palestine once they had thrown out the Turks, but was unaware that the British Government had promised the same territory to the Jews as a national homeland. Lawrence, now a Lieutenant Colonel and well-connected socially and politically, became increasingly disillusioned and frustrated with what he saw as the betrayal of the Arab cause.

In 1922 Lawrence, tired of the public attention focused upon him, left the army and joined the RAF as an aircraftsman under the name of Ross. His real identity was soon discovered, and he joined the Tank Corps at Bovington, this time as Private T.E. Shaw, and bought Clouds Hill cottage as a retreat. In 1925 he rejoined the RAF, and spent the next ten years developing and testing high-speed boats that would form the basis of the air-sea rescue service. Throughout these years he lived in Clouds Hill, returning here whenever he could. In 1935 he was involved in a fatal road accident and died five days later. He was buried in the nearby village of Moreton.

## THE WALK

❶ As you begin the walk, take a moment to seek out the memorial to T.E. Lawrence in the corner of the lay-by.

*There are also information plaques about the tanks and other armoured vehicles that may be seen in the adjoining practice range.*

From the lay-by, with your back to the road, turn left onto a footpath. Follow the footpath, parallel to the road and with the tank range on your right. In 100 yards, look for a headstone on the left, which marks the actual spot where Lawrence met with his accident.

*Lawrence had a fascination with speed, which did not diminish with age. Whilst living at Clouds Hill he bought a Brough Superior SS-100 motorcycle, which he rode at great speed along the Dorset lanes. On 13 May 1935, now aged 47, he rode down this road from Clouds Hill to Bovington Camp to post a telegram. Returning fast, he swerved to avoid two cyclists in a dip in the road, and was thrown from his motorcycle, fracturing his skull. He was taken to the military hospital in Bovington Camp where he died five days later, without regaining consciousness. Conspiracy theories regarding his death immediately surfaced. An unsubstantiated rumour of a car seen near the scene of the accident (a car not mentioned by the two cyclists present at the scene) led to claims that Lawrence's death was deliberately engineered by un-named political enemies.*

*The road from Clouds Hill to Bovington has been straightened and widened since Lawrence's day, and the fateful dip in the lane has disappeared.*

Follow the footpath through the trees for 600 yards, keeping the fence close on your right, to reach a road. Cross a stile on the left and turn left along the main road for 100 yards to a junction. Turn left for 50 yards to Clouds Hill.

*The tiny cottage of Clouds Hill was originally built as a forester's cottage on the Moreton estate. Lawrence discovered it, semi-ruined, in 1923 and decided it would make an ideal retreat. He rented it from the estate owner Henry Frampton, whose forefathers had played a major part in the trial of the Tolpuddle Martyrs (see walk 13), and bought it outright two years later.*

*Lawrence rarely slept in the cottage but used it for evenings and weekends away from his duties at Bovington Camp. The cottage is simple and austere. It was lit by oil lamps and candles, and Lawrence cooked, camp-fire style, over an open fire in the living room. It had no running water until the last year Lawrence lived there, but it provided him with seclusion and privacy. It was here that he wrote 'The Seven Pillars of Wisdom', his account of the Arab campaign and his justification of his views and life, which was published in 1926. In early 1935, Lawrence left the RAF and retired to Clouds Hill, where he entertained his friends. The cottage was given to the National Trust in 1938. It contains many of Lawrence's possessions, his books and records as well as the everyday items he used in his almost monastic lifestyle, and offers a fascinating glimpse into Lawrence's life. Clouds Hill (now a National Trust property) is open mid March to mid October, Thursday to Sunday, from noon until 5 pm. Telephone: 01929 405616.*

❷ To continue the walk, return to the junction with the main road and turn left. Follow the verge along the side of the road for 400 yards. Opposite a side road, turn left into a track. Follow this track for 1 mile through woods and heathland, ignoring all side turns. Cross a bridge and 50 yards later fork right in front of a horse-barrier. Follow the track to reach a long footbridge over the river Frome. Cross the bridge and keep ahead along the track to reach the lane at Moreton. Keep ahead for a few yards, then turn left into a pedestrian-only lane leading to the church of St Nicholas.

*The funeral service of T.E. Lawrence was held in St Nicholas' church on 21 May 1935. Even without Lawrence's own fame, the list of mourners would have guaranteed a strong press presence. The world of politics was represented by Winston Churchill and Lady Nancy Astor, whilst from the arts world were painter Augustus John and writer Robert Graves, the publisher Jonathan Cape and the military historian Liddell Hart. Poet Siegfried Sassoon was so incensed at the intrusion of the press that he took a swing at one photographer with his camera case.*

*The church is well worth a visit. It is very light and airy and contains spectacular glass windows etched by the artist Lawrence Whistler.*

After seeing the church return to the lane and turn left for a few yards to reach a junction.

*The tea-rooms are just on your right.*

❸ Keep ahead along the main road for 100 yards to reach a gate on the right, leading into the churchyard. Lawrence's grave is at the far end of the path.

> **REFRESHMENTS**
>
> The Clouds Hill country pub is a ½ mile (each way) detour from the route. It is a family-friendly, modern pub, with a wide range of food, a children's play area and a beer garden. Telephone: 01929 480206.
>
> There are also two tea-rooms en route at Moreton.

*Lawrence was buried on the same day that the inquest into his death was being held, a reflection that the results of the inquest were perceived to be a foregone conclusion and that there was nothing untoward about the death, conspiracy theories notwithstanding. Lawrence is buried under his own name, despite the fact that he had changed his name to T.E. Shaw by deed poll in 1925. (He took the name Shaw in honour of another close friend of his, George Bernard Shaw.)*
*The garden centre next door has a tea-room.*

To continue the walk, retrace your steps through Moreton and over the long footbridge. Return along the track, passing the horse-barrier on your right and crossing the small footbridge over the tributary stream. When 75 yards past the small footbridge, pass a footpath going off left and in another 75 yards turn right along a side track.

❹ In 300 yards fork left and follow the tree-lined track. Pass a house on the left and then follow the track through a horse-barrier into woods and for a short distance through mature heathland. In the middle of the heath, turn left along a side track leading up into trees. In 400 yards, at a waymark post on the left, fork right up a narrower, stonier path through trees. At the top of the slope keep ahead over a stile and then turn left. Follow the fenced path, marked with yellow posts, as it winds through trees.

*To the right is a tank practice track. It is rare for this to be in use, but you may be lucky (or unlucky, depending on your point of view) and see tanks in operation.*

Continue with the path, the tank course on your right, to reach the road opposite the start of the walk and return to your car. To go to the Clouds Hill pub, turn right and walk down the road for ½ mile, staying close to the verge.

# WALK 15
# STUDLAND BAY AND THE
# REHEARSALS FOR D-DAY, 1944

## Length: 6 miles

*Fort Henry*

**HOW TO GET THERE:** The walk starts from the South Beach National Trust car park in Studland. Studland is on the B3351, 3 miles north of Swanage and 8 miles east of Corfe Castle.

**PARKING:** In the South Beach National Trust car park.

**MAP:** OS Landranger 195 or OS Explorer OL15 (GR 036826).

## INTRODUCTION

This exhilarating walk starts in Studland and visits Fort Henry, overlooking Studland Bay and site of the rehearsals for D-Day. It then crosses Godlingston Heath, passing the unusual Agglestone Rock, before climbing onto Ballard Down and returning past the spectacular Old Harry Rocks. Terrain is easy underfoot, with one short ascent. Route-finding is generally easy.

## HISTORICAL BACKGROUND

Today the long open beaches of Studland Bay are a favourite haunt of holidaymakers, but in the spring of 1944 they were used for a far grimmer purpose, namely rehearsals for the invasion of Europe.

As early as the summer of 1940, while the people of Britain were still celebrating the rescue of the bulk of the British Expeditionary Force from Dunkirk, Churchill told the country that 'wars are not won by evacuations' and set in motion plans for the counter-invasion of Nazi-occupied Europe. When the Japanese attack upon Pearl Harbor in December 1941 drew the USA into the war, he set about convincing the American government that ultimate victory depended upon defeating Germany. Despite initially strong opposition in Washington, Churchill's view prevailed, and as early as January 1942 the first American troops arrived in Britain, starting the build-up of an eventual invasion force.

The wide open beaches of northern France were always the obvious landing site but, despite pressure from the Russians for a second front to be opened up as soon as possible, it was never feasible to invade before 1944. There were huge logistic difficulties involved, over and above gathering and training the necessary troops. For the Germans, too, were well aware that the invasion would occur across the Channel, and had set about building a long line of defences, the 'Atlantic Wall', from Denmark to the Bay of Biscay. To breach this, new weapons and equipment were needed. Huge artificial

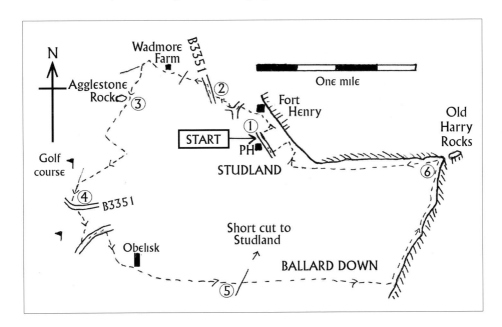

harbours, called Mulberries, were developed to avoid dependence upon enemy ports, and an oil pipeline (Pluto) had to be laid across the floor of the Channel to supply the invasion force.

By the spring of 1944 the men and the equipment were ready, but the latter still needed to be tested under combat conditions. The beaches at Studland Bay bore a close resemblance to the beaches in Normandy, chosen as the invasion site. On 4 April 1944, Operation Smash, a successful rehearsal for the D-Day landings, took place at Studland. Two months later, on 6 June 1944, the long-awaited Allied invasion of occupied Europe commenced.

## THE WALK

❶ From the car park, cross the road and go along the footpath opposite, signed 'Fort Henry and Middle Beach'. Follow the enclosed footpath through a kissing-gate to reach the cliffs above the beach. Turn left above the beach and follow the footpath to Fort Henry.

*The long concrete blockhouses called Fort Henry were built in 1943 by Canadian engineers, part of the defences that protected Studland Bay from German invasion. The main blockhouse is 30 yds long, made of 3 ft thick reinforced concrete, with an embrasure running its full seaward length. Behind the blockhouse is an emplacement for a 4-inch gun battery.*

*Operation Smash was designed to test specific new weapons in combat conditions, especially the amphibious DD (Duplex Drive) tank, known to the troops as 'Donald Duck'. The DD tank was designed to launch itself at sea from a landing craft, propel itself as a boat to land, and then travel inland as a tank. To prepare for Operation Smash, Studland beach was cleared of the mines that had been planted there four years earlier against German invasion. The public had been banned from entering the area, or indeed most of the coastal areas of eastern and southern Britain, for the previous three months, to stop news of the invasion preparations leaking out. In the small hours of 4 April 1944 the operation commenced. Rocket-firing Thunderbolt and Typhoon jet fighters strafed the beach, while a cruiser and several destroyers provided a barrage from the sea. Then, in pitch darkness, the DD tanks were launched 5,000 yards out to sea and made their way onto the beach, whilst live ammunition was fired continually overhead from both directions. The operation was extremely realistic; seven tanks sank and six men of the Royal Dragoons drowned.*

*Operation Smash was watched from the embrasure of Fort Henry by a party including Churchill, Lord Mountbatten (Chief of Combined Operations), and Generals Eisenhower and Montgomery, who would lead the D-Day assaults. Despite the casualties, the operation successfully demonstrated that the new weapons would work, and their inclusion in the D-Day landings was assured. Two weeks later Studland Bay was used for a second rehearsal, this time when men of the Dorset regiment practised amphibious assault from landing craft, again under fire from live ammunition. This rehearsal was watched by King George VI.*

*There is a monument to the soldiers who died in Operation Smash, at the southern end of Fort Henry, overlooking the bay where they drowned.*

From Fort Henry continue along the footpath in the direction signed 'Manor House Hotel'. Follow the footpath to join the road at the gate to Middle Beach car park. Walk up the road away from the car park. At a road junction in 30 yards, bear right. Continue up the road for another 20 yards, then turn right past a metal barrier, down a concrete track signed 'Ferry Road'. The track soon becomes a woodland path.

❷ Follow the path out to a road and turn right for 60 yards, then turn left at a finger-post along an unmade sandy drive. In 200 yards ignore a cross-track but keep ahead along the main track, soon passing through the gates of Wadmore Farm cottages. Bear right and continue along the track, now narrower and less surfaced. Follow the track to go through a kissing-gate beside a metal field gate, then bear left to a finger-post ('Agglestone Rock'). Cross a footbridge and turn left along a sandy path. Follow the path to emerge from trees and in 50 yards, bear left, leaving the main track and going onto a narrow path, aiming at the distinctive boulder of Agglestone Rock seen on the skyline. Follow the path across gorse-covered heath. Wherever a choice occurs, keep on the path aiming at Agglestone Rock. Follow the path, eventually up steps, to the rock.

*Agglestone Rock is a free-standing sandstone boulder, left after the softer rocks that surrounded it had weathered away. Godlingston Heath, on which it stands, is one of Dorset's most extensive heathlands. From Agglestone Rock there are extensive views over Poole Harbour. Some of the landing craft used at D-Day were gathered in this shallow and sheltered harbour, before being taken to their final launching positions. During the war, Poole Harbour was also used to anchor flying boats, long-range amphibious aircraft that provided a vital communications link across the Atlantic. Winston Churchill left from Poole on a flying boat to visit the USA in December 1941, a week after Pearl Harbor, to persuade President Roosevelt to concentrate the war effort against Germany, not Japan.*

❸ From Agglestone Rock, resume your previous direction onto a clear sandy track crossing the hillock ahead. Follow the broad track across the heath to a cross-track at a milestone, with metal gates leading onto a golf course ahead. Turn left and follow the broad sandy track downhill. On reaching a cross-track, ignore a gate and kissing-gate ahead leading onto downs, but instead turn right uphill for 30 yards to a kissing-gate amongst gorse bushes. Go through the double kissing-gate and follow the footpath through gorse and then along the side of a fairway to emerge onto a cross-track in front of golf links. Turn left and follow the footpath into bushes. Go through a kissing-gate and keep ahead to a gate onto a road.

❹ Turn left along the road for 30 yards, then turn right over a stile onto golf links. Keep ahead across the fairway, aiming initially for a bench seen ahead, and then just to the right of a dilapidated barn on the far side of the fairway. Follow a path down through trees to cross a stile, and then go half-right down the field to a stile leading onto a road. Turn left along the broad verge and follow the road for 200 yards. At a bridleway sign, turn right across the road and go up a track to a kissing-gate, leading onto Ballard Down. Keep ahead up a clear track, with bushes initially on your left. Go through a gate and keep ahead on the clear track to reach an obelisk.

*The obelisk was raised to commemorate the introduction of pure drinking water, extracted from the chalk of Ballard Down, into Swanage in 1883. The original was demolished in 1941 to prevent its use as a landmark for German bombers flying to attack Poole, but it was re-erected by men from the Royal Engineers in 1973.*

Keep ahead along the enclosed track to a gate, and then keep ahead on a clear track across Ballard Down.

*In 200 yards you cross a concrete platform set into the grass. This is all that remains of an anti-aircraft gun emplacement, one of several sited on top of Ballard Down to protect Poole Harbour from German bombers. Although the German air force was largely a spent force by 1944, additional anti-aircraft batteries were placed on Ballard Down to protect the VIPs gathered at Fort Henry to watch Operation Smash.*

❺ At a cross-track keep ahead. (Turn left for a shortcut to Studland.)

*The low, tree-covered Brownsea Island can clearly be seen in the middle of Poole Harbour. During 1940 and 1941 this uninhabited island had numerous lights placed on it, to decoy German bombers into thinking it was Poole. As a result, thousands of tons of German bombs destined for Poole were dropped harmlessly onto Brownsea.*

Eventually pass through a gate to reach a trig point. Bear right to pass through a gate and then maintain your previous direction, a fence on your left. Follow the cliff path to Old Harry Rocks.

**REFRESHMENTS**

The Bankes Arms, next to South Beach car park, is an old oak-beamed pub, with a large beer garden, open all day and offering a range of food. Telephone: 01929 450225.

*The Old Harry Rocks are amongst the finest examples of chalk stacks in Britain. A finger of soft chalk rock (Ballard Down) extends out into the sea. Over the millennia water erosion undermined the rock at sea level, cutting firstly caves, then extending those caves right through the rock to create natural arches. Continuing erosion eventually weakened the arch, which collapsed and left a pillar of chalk standing in the sea.*

❻ From Old Harry, walk along a clear track between bushes, the cliff to your right. Follow the clear path out to a green sward and keep ahead, bushes to the left. When you reach a finger-post, signed 'Cliff Path', turn right over a small footbridge and down a sunken path to the beach. Turn left along the front of beach huts. At a white wooden refreshment hut turn left up the track. Follow the track to a road and turn right uphill to reach the Bankes Arms and return to the car park.

# WALK 16
# KIMMERIDGE BAY – TWO THOUSAND YEARS OF INDUSTRY

Length: 7½ miles

*The oil well at Kimmeridge Bay*

| | | |
|---|---|---|
| **HOW TO GET THERE:** The walk starts from the Houns-tout free forestry car park just to the south of Kingston, which is on the B3069, 1 mile south of Corfe Castle. | **PARKING:** In the centre of the village, turn up past the Scotts Arms pub and the church, along a no through road; the car park is 200 yards further on. | **MAP:** OS Landranger 195 or OS Explorer OL15 (GR 954795). |

## INTRODUCTION

This magnificent coastal walk is one of the most spectacular in Dorset. Starting from Kingston, it goes to Swyre Head and then along a ridge to Kimmeridge Bay, with excellent views all the way. From the bay and its oil well, you return along the cliffs to Kingston. Although it is long, the walk is easy underfoot, and route finding is simple. There are no appreciable gradients on the outward route, but the return leg undulates, occasionally steeply.

## HISTORICAL BACKGROUND

Kimmeridge Bay has been an industrial centre for 2,000 years, exploiting the oil shales of the area, and today has one of Britain's few on-shore oil wells.

The Jurassic Coast from Lyme Regis to Swanage is comprised of extravagantly folded bands of rock from the Upper Jurassic and Cretaceous eras. Uniquely on this coast, at Kimmeridge Bay there is a 2 ft thick layer of bituminous shale known as 'oil shale'. This is a shiny stone, jet-black when wet, which has been extracted for millennia, initially because of its attractive appearance, later for fuel.

The Neolithic inhabitants of this region dug out the oil shale where it came near to the surface of the land, and used it to make ornaments. They were aware of its potential as fuel, and there is some evidence that there was a salt manufacturing industry here in Neolithic times, the oil shale being burned to boil sea-water and thus extract salt. When the Romans settled in Dorset in the 1st century AD, they rapidly exploited the Kimmeridge oil shale to manufacture attractive black ornaments, turning it into armlets, cups, rings and pendants in nearby Dorchester and Blandford Forum. Ornaments made from Kimmeridge shale found their way across most of the Roman Empire.

The use of oil shale as fuel was largely forgotten, however, and it was not until the 17th century that it was again extracted on a commercial scale. In the 1630s Sir William Clavell, the wealthiest landowner in the area, developed a factory where locally-mined alum, a chalky mineral, was processed for use in dying and printing. Clavell mined oil shale to fuel his factory. Later a glass works was built in the Kimmeridge Bay area, again

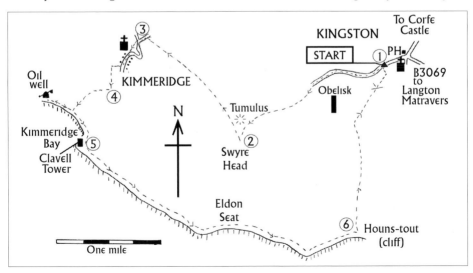

using the oil shale as fuel. This mining remained on a small scale until 1848, when the Bituminous Fuel Co of Weymouth was formed to extract the oil shale commercially, and in 1858 a contract was gained to provide natural gas to light the city streets of Paris.

After the Second World War, the Kimmeridge Bay oil was exploited commercially. Although it was soon surpassed in size by the Poole Harbour field, it is still in commercial production today.

## THE WALK

❶ From the car park, turn left and continue along the quiet road, walking away from Kingston.

*Corfe Castle can be seen to your right, dominating the countryside and blocking the strategic Corfe Gap, the only feasible road route through the Purbeck ridge.*

Continue along the road for ¾ mile, until you reach a parking area. Turn left through a gate, signed to Encombe House and Lower Encombe, and keep ahead to a pedestrian gate beside a metal field gate (signed 'Swyre Head 1'). Follow the clear track up the field and go through a kissing-gate in the top corner. Keep ahead, a wall on your right, along an airy track with great views down to the sea at Chapman's Pool, with St Aldhelm's Head beyond. Continue, the slope close on your left, eventually leaving the wall and bearing left to a distinctive tumulus ahead.

*This huge tumulus is a burial mound dating from Neolithic times, some 4,000 years ago. The dead who had importance to a community, either political or religious, were buried in stone tombs, on top of which a huge mound of earth, or tumulus, was raised. It was common practice to raise these on prominent places so that they would be visible for miles and thus provide striking proof of the existence and power of the community. The Neolithic tribe who dominated this area around 2000 BC were the first people to exploit the oil shales of nearby Kimmeridge Bay.*

Keep ahead to a stone bench at the end of Swyre Head.

❷ After admiring the view, turn your back to the bench and walk with the fence close on your left. Ignore a stile on the left leading to a permissive path but continue ahead, passing the trig point, to a waymarked gate in the corner of the wall. Keep ahead, the wall on your left, and follow the path along the summit of the ridge. Go through a gate and along an enclosed track, to pass through another gate into a field. Continue ahead, a wall on your left, through two fields, soon on a clear track. Follow the track down the side of a third field to reach a lane.

❸ Turn left down the lane for 80 yards to a road junction. Cross the road to a stile beside a finger-post ('Kimmeridge ¼'). Follow the path steeply downhill, go through a kissing-gate and down a path along the side of the churchyard. Leave the path through a second kissing-gate and keep ahead down the main street of Kimmeridge, passing the combined post office, stores and tea-room. Immediately past the last house on the right (no 20), turn right over a stile at a finger-post. Go down the side of a field, the fence on your right. In the bottom corner cross stiles and a footbridge and turn left, winding along the edge of a large field. At the bottom corner of the field go through a gate and turn left. Follow the field boundary along two fields to reach a road.

❹ Turn right along the road to reach Kimmeridge Bay at a two-way finger-post. Turn right along the cliff edge to the oil well.

*There is a band of oil-bearing rock 1,500 ft below ground at this point. During the Second World War attempts were made to extract the oil, but the depth made the task too difficult for it to be viable. Improvements in drilling techniques and machinery after the war led British Petroleum Co to try again, this time successfully, and oil was first extracted here in 1959. A small oil well has operated here ever since, using the distinctive 'nodding donkey' pump.*

*In the 1970s oil was discovered at Wytch Farm, on the southern shores of Poole Harbour, with much deeper deposits being found nearby in the next decade. Until recent discoveries in Russia, Poole Harbour was the largest on-shore oil field in Europe. Although the Kimmeridge Bay oil field is small by comparison to Poole, it is still commercially viable. Currently 80 barrels (12,720 litres) of oil are extracted daily. It is collected every fortnight and taken by tanker to the BP oil depot at Wytch Farm, and then exported via Southampton.*

Retrace your steps along the cliff to the finger-post and keep ahead, following the cliff path past houses and down to the beach.

*Anti-tank traps and a pill box are still clearly visible on the beach, left over from the Second World War, when there was an imminent threat of Nazi invasion to the whole of this south coast.*

Continue up steps and follow the cliff path past a car park and then past toilets. At a tarmac access road turn right down towards the bay, through more anti-tank traps. At the bottom of the slope, just before black huts, turn left up steps.

*Sir William Clavell, who started to mine the oil shale in the 1630s, tried unsuccessfully to develop Kimmeridge Bay as a port, building a stone jetty at this point with the hope of shipping the produce of his alum works from here. The Clavell family had been the major landowners in the Kimmeridge area for five centuries. Their family seat, Smedmore House, is a mile inland. The project was unsuccessful, as the bay is too exposed to provide safe all-season anchorage.*

> **REFRESHMENTS**
>
> The Scotts Arms in Kingston is a quaint old pub, with many nooks and alcoves and a large beer garden, with fine views over Corfe Castle. It has a good range of bar food and a separate dining room. Telephone: 01929 480270.
>
> There is also a tea-room halfway round the walk, at Kimmeridge.

❺ Climb the steps to reach Clavell Tower.

*Clavell Tower was built in 1820 by the Rev John Clavell, a member of the dominant local family. It is a cylindrical tower, with a mixture of classical motifs and Tuscan columns. It was built primarily as a folly, although there is some evidence that the parapet on the top was specifically designed to support a telescope, Clavell being a keen amateur astronomer.*

Continue along the clifftop path for 2 miles, eventually passing over Eldon Seat and then descending to a walled gully before climbing steps. Continue up the cliff to reach a stone bench on top of Houns-tout.

❻ From the bench, turn left across a stile and continue along the ridge, a wall on your right. Follow the ridge for ¾ mile, crossing a second stile, to finally reach a third stile beside a field gate.

*The obelisk seen on the hillside to the left is in the grounds of the Encombe estate, and was raised by the owners, the Scott family. John Scott, later first Earl of Eldon, was Lord Chancellor to Pitt the Younger, and bought Encombe in 1806. The house was extensively rebuilt and the grounds were remodelled by the famous landscape gardener Humphrey Repton. In line with the vogue of the time, mock Grecian temples and obelisks were placed at strategic points to enhance the landscape.*

Cross the stile and keep ahead along a clear track through woods. In 150 yards, at the gates to Hill View Cottage, keep ahead along a surfaced track. After 50 yards, at a T-junction, bear right and 30 yards further on, at a junction of several tracks, fork right, signed 'Kingston ½'. Follow the track for ¼ mile and then turn left back to the car park. (The Scotts Arms pub is a further ¼ mile down the lane.)